Dating

Making Your Own Choices

KAREN DOCKREY

BROADMAN PRESS
Nashville, Tennessee

© Copyright 1987 ● Broadman Press
All Rights Reserved
ISBN: 0-8054-5345-8
4253-45

Dewey Decimal Classification: 646.7
Subject Heading: DATING (SOCIAL CUSTOMS)
Library of Congress Catalog Number: 86-30985
Printed in the United States of America

Chapters 3, 5, and 9 are adapted from articles in *event* Sept. 1986, Feb. 1987,
Mar. 1986, and Feb. 1986, and *equipping youth,* 10/86. © Copyright 1985, 1986
The Sunday School Board of the Southern Baptist Convention. All rights reserved.
Used by permission.

Library of Congress Cataloging-in-Publication Data

Dockrey, Karen, 1955-
    Dating: making your own choices.

    Summary: Addresses questions and concerns about
dating from a Christian perspective.
    1. Dating (Social customs)—Juvenile literature.
2. Dating (Social customs)—Religious aspects—
Christianity—Juvenile literature.   [1. Dating
(Social customs) 2. Christian life]   I. Title.
HQ801.D63   1987   646.7'7   86-30985
ISBN 0-8054-5345-8 (pbk.)

To

D. W. and Beverly Dockrey

who beautifully demonstrate their lifelong love

THANKS

to the youth of Bluegrass Baptist Church
for reading and responding to the chapters in this book

to youth across the Southern Baptist Convention
who shared their dating experiences and ideas

to Bill, for being my favorite date

Contents

It's Your Choice 7

1. Dating: Finding Lifelong Love 9

2. Dates: Who to Choose 18

3. Beginnings: Make a Good Impression 26

4. Dates: Enjoy Them 33

5. Closeness: How It Grows 40

6. Sex: God's Good Gift 48

7. No Dates? Don't Give Up Yet 60

8. Problems: Handle Them Positively 69

9. Parents: An Asset Worth Considering 77

10. Love: Have You Found It? 85

11. Breaking Up: Minimize the Pain 95

12. Marriage: Recognize When You're Ready 103

It's Your Choice

"What if nobody asks me out?"
"What if she turns me down?"
"What will we talk about?"
"What if I do something dumb?"
"Where do I sit in the car?"
"What if I don't kiss right?"
"How far is too far?"
"How can we grow closer?"

There's a lot to worry about isn't there! Anything important is worth asking about. But rather than worrying over your questions, let your questions drive you to action. Rather than waiting for something to happen, choose to make your love life great. Learn how to meet people, to talk, to listen, to understand, to love. Refuse to go out with just anyone, to put up with bad treatment, to settle for less than the best. Choose to find solutions to your dating problems and then use the solutions you discover. It won't be easy, but it's worth the effort.

Growing a happy love life is up to you. Only you can choose the person you'll date, where you'll go, what you'll do, and how good your love life will be. Nobody else can do it for you, not your parents, not your friends, not your dates.

That may make you feel proud or overwhelmed! But be assured that there's plenty of help available: God is ready and waiting to advise you, to encourage you, and to equip you. Because He created love, He knows the best ways to show it, the type people who will make you happiest, the ways to solve problems, and the actions that will help you grow close to your special someone. He has great plans for your love life. But you must choose God's plans. He will never force His way on you.

I have written this book to help you discover God's guidelines and some concrete actions you can take to improve your love life. I challenge you to learn all you can, to understand what will make you happy, and to make smart choices about dating, sex, and marriage. You and your dates will be glad you did!

A few technical items about this book:

• The names in all situations have been changed to protect the privacy of the persons involved. If you see your name, I haven't been watching you, I just like your name!

• All the situations apply to both guys and girls. To avoid the awkward *he/she,* I have used *he* and *she* interchangeably. Put yourself in each situation and change the sexes to match you.

• *Sweetheart* has been used to designate girl friend, boyfriend, honey, the one you like, and so on.

• You'll notice three boldface cues throughout the chapters:

Challenge, Read On, and **Think.** These encourage you to apply that section's truths to your unique situation.

God wants to teach you how to enjoy dating (and waiting). As you learn His ways, ask God for courage to obey them. Watch, talk with, and learn from other Christians who are already living His kind of love. Keep asking, reading, and learning until you understand and can live God's dating and marriage truths. Growing a godly love life is an adventure you won't want to miss!

1
Dating:
Finding Lifelong Love

"I just fell in love. I couldn't help myself."

So begins one of the most convincing myths ever devised. Falling in love sounds great, but its success depends on where you fall. The main problem with falling is that you can get hurt. You have a slight chance of falling in the right spot and finding someone suited for you. But more likely, you'll enjoy the fall but not the landing. Love is more like a journey down a scenic road than like a fall off a mountain.

Rather than something you "fall into," real love is a series of choices: You choose whom to date, how long to date that person, and whether to date several people or one at a time. You choose whether to treat your dates well or to use them and whether to be good to yourself or to settle for being used. You choose whether to marry, whom to marry, when to marry, and how long your marriage will last. You decide how happy your love life will be.

Dating is one of the best ways to make these love choices. Rather than a haphazard, hit-or-miss operation, dating can be a conscious effort to find and enjoy the person God has for you. The person who said, "I couldn't help myself" chose to bury her brain for the sake of feelings. There's nothing wrong with feelings—God created them. But He did not intend for you to base your future on feelings alone. Let your mind be involved to be sure your heart is right.

While you are dating someone you:

    experience how comfortable you are together

    discover how easy or hard it is to solve problems together

    recognize what makes him happy and what frustrates him

notice how she acts in all kinds of situations
talk about every imaginable subject
watch whether he lives what he says he believes
encounter her good and bad habits
find things that please and that anger you.

You decide if you want to live with both the pleasing and the frustrating qualities of this person. You decide if you want to go through every life experience with him, if you want to commit to lifelong love—marriage.

As you follow God's leadership in dating, you'll learn to love God's way. God's love builds a foundation for happiness that will last your whole life. It will help you create an enjoyable dating life and and a lasting marriage. It can even make you happy while you're not dating!

Challenge: Learn how to grow deep and lasting love. Let your heart, mind, and spirit work together to find true love.

So What Is Dating?

We can define dating as a noun as: 1. The process by which one selects a spouse. 2. A set of prearranged times together with someone of the opposite sex. As a verb, dating means going out with the opposite sex to enjoy each other, to get to know each other, and to evaluate whether you're suited for marriage.

Why date? In addition to choosing a life mate, youth date to:
Share feelings, thoughts, hopes
     Practice for marriage
          Enjoy the opposite sex
               to find love
                    To have fun!

Finding True Love

Since finding love is one of the main reasons to date, how do we go about it? What do these say about how to find love?

CINDERELLA: One enchanting evening is all you need to tell if you are in love. It guarantees happiness.

Truth: Lots of time together in a variety of experiences helps you know how happy you will be together. See Chapter 4 for ways to get to know each other and Chapter 10 to tell if you're in love.

FAIRY TALES: Love always ends up happily ever after.

Truth: Romantic feelings are like dessert—they taste great, but they can't nourish a relationship. True love needs the meat and potatoes of commitment, work, and talking.

SOAP OPERAS: When you get tired of one sweetheart, its over. Change to another.

Truth: All new relationships have lots of romance. This fire of excitement gradually settles to glowing embers. A couple can either stoke the fire and restart the flame or let it smoulder and go out. Switching to a different sweetheart gives, at best, a few more months of burning passion. Then the fire goes out again. It makes more sense to add fuel to the original fire than to start new fires every time the flame dies down. Happiness comes through nurturing one relationship throughout life.

MOVIES AND MUSIC: If you like somebody, go to bed with them.

Truth: Sex requires a strong relationship; it cannot put one together. In fact, sex can be used to avoid a close, caring relationship. Movies and music don't admit that sex outside of marriage usually creates more problems than it solves. They paint a picture of easy pleasure. But true sexual pleasure comes through commitment. In real life good sex takes a lifetime to perfect and works best in a secure, happy relationship. God calls this relationship marriage.

LOVE STORIES: Love is something you fall into.

Truth: Though emotional happiness starts most loves, only commitment can keep it going. Love lasts when each person decides to make it last, not by falling in the right place.

So Where Are the Answers?

If none of these has the straight story on love, who does? *Jesus Christ.* He lived the pattern for a fabulous love life.

"Jesus? He didn't date! How can He teach me how to ask someone out and grow a great romance?"

Good romance grows when the actions of Jesus are imitated. The ways He treated people, responded to problems, and built relationships work marvelously in dating. As Hebrews 4:14-16 explains, Jesus understands our dating feelings, helps us solve our problems, and rejoices with our happiness.

Jesus' actions teach that:
- Every person needs respect.
- Persons are to be loved, not used.
- Women and men are equally important.
- Deception (including using people and dating someone you really don't like) has no place in dating.
- When guilty of sexual sin, seek forgiveness and refuse to participate again.
- Enjoy God, life, and each other.

Bible verses that apply to dating include:

"Well, whatever you do, whether you eat or drink [or date] do it all for God's glory" (1 Cor. 10:31).

"Do not use harmful words, but only helpful words, the kind that build up and provide what is needed, so that what you say will do good to those who hear you" (Eph. 4:29).

"In this matter, then, no man should do wrong to his fellow Christian or take advantage of him. We have told you this before, and we strongly warned you that the Lord will punish those who do that" (1 Thess. 4:6).

"So let us adopt any custom that leads to peace and our mutual improvement" (Rom. 14:19, *Jerusalem Bible*).

"Don't let the world around you squeeze you into its own mould, but let God remake you so that your whole attitude of mind is changed. Thus you will prove in practice that the will of God [is] good, acceptable to him and perfect" (Rom. 12:2, Phillips).

"Instead, by speaking the truth in a spirit of love, we must grow up in every way to Christ, who is the head" (Eph. 4:15).

"Fill your minds with those things that are good and that deserve praise: things that are true, noble, right, pure, lovely, and honorable" (Phil. 4:8).

As demonstrated by the above samples, God's Word, the Bible, contains plenty of advice for great dating. He knows you want a relationship with someone special because He gave you that yearning. Dating His way brings joy unspeakable and a marriage even better.

Challenge: How would living each of these Bible verses improve your dating life?

Dating for the Best Reasons

You have control of your dating life. Be good to yourself by dating the right people for the right reasons!

Youth suggested these wrong reasons for dating:

  To make someone jealous or get back at that someone

  To avoid hurting someone's feelings by saying no

  To find security (opens you up to being used)

  Because you're too timid to say no

  To cure loneliness or unhappiness

  Because your parents or friends like that person

  To prove independence

  To gain popularity or impress someone

  To use/take advantage of the other person

  To get sex.

Youth suggested these right reasons for dating:

  Because you're attracted to someone and want to be with him

  To find out your likes and dislikes in people

  To have fun

  To get to know someone you're interested in

  To learn how to relate to a sweetheart

  To grow closer to somebody you care for.

Think: What are your top three reasons for dating? Which negative reason are you most prone to? How might dating for this negative reason harm you and your potential date?

When Can I Begin My Love Life?

The best time to start dating is when you're ready. As youth and their parents suggest: "Youth should start dating when they are old enough to accept responsibility and mature enough to act right on a date." Most youth say fifteen or sixteen is the right age for beginning to date. But you are unique: What's right for your friends might be too late or too early for you. Much depends on who is asking and where the date will be. There's a big difference between going to a college dance with a twenty-two-year-old and attending the local softball game with someone your age. Talk it over with your parents. Honestly assess yourself and the person you want to date.

If you and your parents decide that you're not quite ready for single dating, the relationship is not doomed. With parental permission, try:

Inviting the person to your house to study.

Talking on the phone.

Including the person in a family cookout.

Seeing the person at group functions.

Inviting the person to your house may seem dull. But consider its advantages:

• As your parents get to know your sweetheart, they tend to trust him.

• The way the person gets along with your family helps you evaluate your "rightness" for each other.

• The way you get along with his parents helps you know how well you really like the person.

The best news is that you don't have to wait until you're dating to start your love life. Learn now how to show love through talking with people, solving problems, and sharing your feelings. Practice on your friends, your parents, your sisters and brothers, the kid next door. Get to know persons of both sexes at church, at school, wherever groups gather. The more you practice loving now, the better you'll be when you date.

Think: Dating is not the only place to find love. In fact, unless you already have love in your life—love for family, love for God—you'll have a hard time loving a sweetheart. Why?

What Do People Want in a Sweetheart?

Guys listed these characteristics they like in girls:

Friendship   Easy to talk to   Fun to be with

Good looks	Good personality	Smart
Not boring	Nice, not snobby	Not a druggie/drinker
Good morals	Not an airhead	Treats you right
Common sense	Talents	Relaxes
Shows emotion	Romantic	Funny
Christian	Nice body	Easygoing

Guys avoid the cute-but-nothing-else model. Though they want someone attractive on the outside, they want personality inside. They also stress the importance of being yourself. *"She might be afraid to admit that she likes fishing instead of football. Fishing might be just what I want to do, but unless we tell each other, we'll miss enjoying together something we both like. I think that's what causes divorces; we don't let our true selves be known until after the wedding."*

Think: Some guys said there aren't enough good girls around. *"They all smoke and drink,"* said one. *"I don't want a girl like that. Where are the ones who live right?"* Where are they?

Girls listed these characteristics they like in guys:

Fun to be with	Good looks	Good Personality
Considerate	Not in love with themselves	
A good reputation	Friendship	Respects me
Intelligence	Sense of humor	Acts like a gentleman
Sensitive	Kind	Nice build
Caring	Christian	Responsible
Good attitude	Talkative	Not cheating on you

Girls seemed to want a guy who isn't afraid to show his feelings. Rather than a macho guy, they want someone who is sensitive, talkative, and real. *"I want a guy who has both physical and emotional strength, someone who can speak what he feels and not let anyone hold him back,"* said one.

Think: Girls tend to see romance as security whereas some guys feel tied down by it. Why do you think this is so?

What Are the Differences?

The differences between individuals are usually greater than the differences between sexes. Rather than focusing on "how the opposite sex thinks," learn how the person you are interested in thinks. Each of us is unique and special.

The guys and girls I surveyed agreed that the three most important characteristics are:

1. Looks,
2. Personality,
3. Fun to be with.

You likely have an image of a perfect person with these three characteristics, and that person is not you. But don't let this image deceive you. Here's where the true differences come in. Each person likes a slightly different variety of looks, personality, and fun. You match someone's dream perfectly.

How are these very different people beautiful, full of personality, and fun?

Tony is the life of the party. He tells jokes and keeps everyone laughing. His tousled hair and freckles give him that mischeivous look that Jill loves.

Gina has a compliment for everyone. She makes you feel so important by listening to you and understanding your feelings. Alan cherishes her sensitivity and concern.

Ric is quiet in a group but genuine and adventuresome. Every new day delights and challenges him. He and Emma watch for a new friend or new bit of understanding everywhere they go. The simple things take on a whole new meaning when Ric is around.

Challenge: The key to finding someone who will love you is not to match that someone's checklist of desired qualities. The key is to be yourself. The lists help you notice qualities that would make you more the person you want to be.

Read On: Even the most attractive person feels ugly, at least occasionally. Exercise as instructed in Chapter 7 to notice and believe the beauty God gave you.

Choose a Happy Love Life

The people you date today influence your tomorrows. Each experience teaches you better how to love or erects barriers to closeness. How did these choices enhance or harm future dating and marriage for these people:

"I'll never forget the first time I went all the way. Not that it was that great, it was just the first time. The problem is, it was not with my wife. That memory seems to make us less close. We love each other, and she has forgiven me. I just wish I had made love only with her."

"Ivan tried so hard to impress me that he almost killed me. He drank to show what a man he was, and then instead of letting me drive, he forced his way into the driver's seat. 'I can handle it,' he bragged, just before crashing into the guardrail. I spent six weeks in the hospital for his show of manliness."

"I remember how sweet it was learning how to date and flirt. I was so nervous and did some dumb things. But Leonard liked me anyway. My memories of him are such good ones, and I often wonder what he's up to now. I'm forever indebted to him for accepting me fully and for teaching me that I am loveable."

Challenge: Why you date, who you date, and what you do on your dates will bring tremendous happiness or crippling frustration. Build a foundation for happy love by choosing wisely.

Think: Your dating life (including how you react when you don't have a date) reflects what you believe about yourself and God. What conclusions would people draw by watching you?

2
Dates: Who to Choose

Youth of several ages and backgrounds recommend you ask the following questions about people you want to date.

Is this person interesting to you?
- Do you or would you enjoy spending time with this person?
- Would you like to know this person better?
- Would you consider marrying this person?

Do you know this person?
- Do you already know a lot about this person?
- Are you certain you can trust this person?
- Will this person treat you right?

Do you share the same beliefs?
- Is this person a Christian?
- Do her actions match what she says she believes?
- Are his morals, personality, and friends the type you want?

Do you have more in common than you have differences?
- Are your personalities and interests similar?
- Can you be yourselves around each other?
- Is this person close to your age and experience level?

Is this person beautiful?
- Is this person physically attractive to you? (Beauty comes in assorted varieties!)
- Is she even prettier on the inside than she is on the outside?
- Do you like his attitudes and values?

Does this person treat you and others well?
- Does he treat you well when his friends are around?

- Does she refrain from gossip and backbiting?
- Is he considerate of past sweethearts?

Does this person have a good reputation?

- Do other people have positive things to say about him?
- Does she have a good reputation at school? At church?
- Do adults like him?

The more yes answers you gave to these questions, the greater likelihood he is a good choice.

Youth stress that you get to know the people you feel attracted to, at least a little bit, before going out with them. They suggest you talk to them and watch what they do. This helps you discover how much fun you'd have together, how they would treat you, and what is important to them.

A Note About "Picking Up" Dates: Going out with someone you don't know can be boring, surprising, or downright dangerous. Girls have been raped or worse by going out with someone they've met just once.

I Wish!

"I'd love to date someone who meets all those qualifications. But the people who ask me out treat me really rotten. I guess I have no choice."

You *do* have a choice! Too often youth approach dating as something that happens to them, rather than something they control. Your decisions, words, and actions help determine the type people you date. You can attract the ones who will treat you well.

"But he's the best I can get!"

Refuse to fall into this trap. You're a quality person. When you believe that, others will too! They'll treat you as God's masterpiece.

Challenge: Talk to God about your dating life. Since He created love, He knows who can make you happy. Ask God to help you recognize dates that will be perfect for you.

Date Selection Tips

Youth suggest these tips for choosing dates:

Meet many different people from whom you can choose. This helps you discover the type of person you want to date.

Decide what interests you about this person. Be sure it is more than just looks or status.

Rather than choosing from who's available, think about the kind of person you want. If you're already dating "second best," "number one" probably won't notice you when he comes along.

Talk about beliefs, dreams, ideas, and goals for the future. Find somebody who matches you.

Don't compromise your standards just to get a date.

Notice who the person's friends are and how they act.

Use your head as well as your heart.

Think: Similarity between you and your date lessens the likelihood of fights and makes those fights easier to resolve. How would a close match in age, heritage, race, interests, views toward money, and beliefs increase dating happiness?

Challenge: As you decide whom to date, you may find that everybody has a different opinion about who is right for you. Your best sources of advice are Christians with happy marriages. Notice the couples who communicate well, have fun, and show affection. Watch how they live out the Bible. As you imitate them, ask God to develop even deeper love in your marriage.

Dating Myths

Knowing the truths about dating relationships can keep you from creating problems for yourself.

Myth 1: Dating brings instant happiness.

Fact: We all long for that special someone who will love us thoroughly and whom we can love in return. We feel that, when we find this someone, all our problems will be solved and we will live happily ever after. But this only works for people who are happy already. Two unhappy persons don't make a happy couple: They become two messed-up people struggling to find happiness.

Myth 2: You can never be whole until you are united with your "other half."

Fact: God created you good and complete. He will guide you in your choice of someone to love and marry or help you be happy as a single person. Jesus—God in human form—was single. What better model of wholeness and happiness can we have?

Myth 3: It doesn't matter who you date as long as you marry the right kind of person.

Fact: Even if you never marry the date, that person affects you today. A sweetheart influences you more than any other person because you tend to become like those you spend the most time with. Each relationship you choose brings you closer to or further from the person God wants you to be.

Think: What have you done for God as a result of your date's influence? What have you hesitated to say or do about your beliefs because you feared it would offend your date?

Myth 4: Religion is a personal matter and doesn't make that much difference in dating and marriage.

Fact: What you believe determines how you act, what you think, and how you treat other people. These certainly affect how easy it is to get along with a sweetheart, how many fights you have, and how happy your romance will be. Whether we are conscious of it or not, the beliefs we were raised with, or which we accepted on our own, impact all of what we do and say.

Date Only Christians?

Mandy, a committed Christian, married someone from the Muslim religion. She didn't think it would matter because he said those beliefs no longer meant anything to him. Besides he was so handsome and considerate. He treated her so specially. Friends envied her for catching such a good man.

A few years after their daughter was born, Mandy's husband announced that he wanted to move back to his home country. Mandy, ready for a new adventure, agreed. The adventure became a nightmare. In his country, men owned their wives. She was required to do whatever he said. She could not even go out with her friends or pick up her children at school without her husband's permission. Mandy felt trapped and terrified. Religion made a lot of difference now.

There are two strong longings in your life: for God and for a sweetheart. When you let the second take priority over the first, you create dating and marriage problems. God knows that only those who love Him can best love each other. That's why He recommends that Christians date Christians. Second Corinthians 6:14-15 explains that close relationships between a Christian and non-Christian can never be completely happy.

When Christians find themselves attracted to non-Christians, they often rephrase their commitment to God: *"God will understand. I know He said not to enter close relationships with non-Christians, but this guy is different. He is so attractive and treats me so well."*

Things certainly seem happy. Why blow such a good relationship just because he's not a Christian? What looks good now can't last without God. God thinks of the future as well as the present. He knows that dating is always fun in the beginning. But as you relax together, the problems start.

"But it doesn't make that much difference who I date. After all, I'm not going to marry him. We're just having fun!"

Having fun together is great. But once you date someone, you either keep dating or break up. If you stay firm on your commitment to marry a Christian, breaking up is your only option. Why start a relationship that has to end? Have your fun at the friendship level.

"But what's the harm in dating a non-Christian? Even if we do break up someday, can't we enjoy getting to know each other now?"

Dating non-Christians has three disadvantages:

1. Because every date is a potential mate, your friendship with a non-Christian may develop into romantic love. You may then be unwilling to break off the relationship. Love can talk you out of what you know is right. As Jeremiah 17:9 explains, "Who can understand the human heart? There is nothing else so deceitful."

2. Dating a nonbeliever puts a Christian in the position of deciding between God's way and the sweetheart's way. Christian youth who date non-Christians seldom mean to turn away from God. They sim-

ply, gradually, let someone else become more important than God. As love for a nonbeliever grows, the Christian tries harder to please her, even when it means ignoring God.

3. You are less likely to notice or be asked out by a Christian if you are already dating a non-Christian.

"But the Christians at my school are so dull! Many non-Christian guys treat me better than they do. I'd rather have someone with personality!"

Christianity is not a guarantee of compatibility any more than maleness guarantees compatibility with every female. Because God loves all people, the people who love Him back come in all varieties. Choose a Christian who matches you. Christianity, though an essential element, is not the only element. There are also looks, interests, talents, goals, and personality. Hint: If you don't see a Christian sweetheart who matches you, don't give up. God will guide you as you look for someone.

" 'Date only Christians' still sounds so restrictive. Doesn't God love everybody? Isn't He for freedom?"

God is definitely for love and freedom. But He understands that though He loves everybody, not everybody loves Him back. Only those who love Him are willing to obey Him. The more closely a person obeys God, the better he'll get along with others. We think we're finding greater dating freedom when we convince ourselves that God is being unreasonable. But we end up with less freedom: Rather than waiting for a sweetheart who loves us completely, as only a Christian can, we restrict ourselves to what looks good now. We cheat ourselves out of God's best.

"But I can witness to her! She'll change for me!"

Evangelistic dating never works very well, unless you aren't a Christian. Your non-Christian date has a better chance of evangelizing you than the other way around. Gradually she'll "witness" to you about the advantages of ignoring God. She won't do this consciously, but because you want to please her, you'll do as she does. Drawing someone away from God is easier than drawing someone to Him.

Your girl friend may be genuinely seeking answers. In that case, it is certainly right to witness to her. Ask questions like: "What do you think God is like?" "What makes you doubt He is real?" "What makes you think He might be real?" "What do you think about church? Christianity?" "Did you know that Jesus can become your best friend?" Walk her toward an understanding of God and Christianity. The book *Getting to Know God* (Broadman Press, 1984) can help.

If she continues to resist Christianity after a week or two, back off from the relationship. The longer you date, the easier it becomes to make excuses for her lack of Christian belief and life-style: "She'll change later; God won't mind me dating her."

Be honest enough to admit that your main motivation for dating her is not witnessing. You emphasize her good looks and sweet personality and tack on the "I'll witness to her" as a bargain with God. If God leads her to salvation through you, marvelous! But if not, recognize excuses you may be making.

"She became a Christian! I guess all is OK now, right!"

Hopefully. But realize that she may have "become a Christian" just to please you. Be sure she's growing in her faith. You want not just a churchgoer but a Christian to whom Jesus is number one. Find someone who lives her faith, who brings you joy, who helps you understand God better.

Challenge: Sometimes you won't know if your date is a growing Christian, or a Christian at all, until you date a few times. Make it a point to talk about Christianity by the third date. Ways to bring up the topic include: "What do you think Jesus' teachings say about this?" "What do you think about Christianity?" "Tell me about you and God." "What do you think is best about living the Christian life? Hardest?"

Think: First Kings 11:2-4 warns us not to marry unbelievers because they will draw us away from God. How could dating a nonbeliever also draw us away from God?

Let's Trust God Enough to Date Only Believers

Psalm 37:4 explains that when you trust God for happiness, He will give you your heart's desire, that includes a sweetheart who will make you delightfully happy. Trust God to guide you to find the Christian sweetheart He's developing for you. If you don't recognize her yet, just wait a bit. While you're waiting, dream a little about what she will be like. Jot down your image of the ideal. Talk with God about what He would like added or deleted from your image. Then don't settle for less than God's best:

1. Refuse to let a difficult situation talk you out of God's ideal. These include: "There just aren't any cute Christians!" "The only thing wrong with him is that he's not a Christian."

2. Rather than comparing person against person, compare your date against the ideal. "He shows his faith in everyday life" is better than "He's the best person I've ever dated."

3. Look toward the future. One of the devil's most effective strategies is to force you to concentrate on the present: "If you don't start dating today, you never will!" Trust God's timing.

Challenge: Notice the married people in your church: Who seems to live and enjoy their Christianity best—the ones who married Christians or the ones who married non-Christians?

3
Beginnings: Make a Good Impression

"I've got my eye on her but I don't know how to meet her!"
"Once I meet her, what do we talk about?"
"How can I let him know I like him?"
"He has finally asked me out, and I'm so nervous! What should I do and say on the first date to be sure he keeps liking me?"

How can you attract that person who interests you? These actions can show your interest and overcome the shyness you may have about talking to each other.

Smile. Smiling at the right time can let him know you are interested. Use your eyes and words to smile too. Smiling says, "Who you are and what you do pleases me."

Say hello. Let him know how glad you are to see him.

Begin the conversation. Because she is probably as shy as you are, make the first move! Ask, "When do you work next?" "How did the class respond to your report?" Then really listen.

Concentrate on the other person. Work toward making her comfortable by asking questions. Focusing on her helps you forget your discomfort long enough to enjoy getting to know her.

Listen. Listen to every word he says. Notice what makes him happy, what frustrates him, what he'll be doing tomorrow. When you listen you are saying, "You are important to me."

Respond. After you've heard what he says, respond in ways that show you care. When he tells you he missed the soccer goal, don't boast that you didn't miss! Instead express your care: "I know you were disappointed. What did you do then?"

Remember and say so. Once you've listened, remember to ask again. "What grade did you get?" Let him know what impresses you: "I thought you did a great job on the report."

Read On: Did you know that God is the best matchmaker there is? Read Psalm 37:4. Let God help you recognize whether the one you have your eye on will make you happy!

Risk Showing You Care

"How should I say it? Will she say yes? . . . probably not. I'm sure she won't go out with me. But isn't it worth a try? . . . I don't want to offend her by asking. She'd rather have someone more handsome and popular. Maybe I should just ask Gail. It won't be such a big deal if she says no."

Thoughts like these go through the mind of almost every male as he tries to work up his courage to ask for a date. Even the most attractive and confident guys struggle, at least occasionally, with asking girls out. Fearing a refusal, many simply don't ask or ask their second choice: *"A refusal confirms that she doesn't like me. Not asking maintains hope."*

If you're waiting to be asked out, let him know you care in some of the ways suggested. His inaction may mean he's not sure if you like him.

If you are the asker, take the risk! Watch for hints that she cares and believe them. If you aren't sure, ask anyway. She may say yes! And if she doesn't, at least you'll know. You can turn your attention to someone else.

Think: Many youth use the "ask someone to ask her if she wants to go out with me" method. What are the advantages and disadvantages of this system?

Sample Date Requests

Find the flaws in this date request:
"What are you doing Friday night?"
"Nothing, why?"

"Oh, I was just wondering, I know you probably don't want to, but . . . would you like to go out or something?"

"Yes, I would."

"OK, I'll pick you up at seven."

"Great! See you then."

Though she said yes, this date request failed in three ways:

1. By asking *"What are you doing Friday night,"* he forced her to commit herself to an answer before he let her know what he wanted. Even if she had something planned, she might be able to reschedule her plans or change the night of the date. And if she didn't want to go but had nothing planned, she had no "out."

Hint 1: If guys ask this question, respond, "I'm not sure yet. Why do you ask?"

Hint 2: If someone asks you out and you don't want to go, simply say, "No, thank you." Its kinder than any excuse.

2. He said, *"You probably don't want to."* But she did! He didn't need to put himself down. Let her decide whether she wants to go.

3. He never said where they'd be going or when they'll be back. She doesn't know whether to dress for a dusty football game or a fancy dinner. Without knowing the details, her parents are less likely to let her go.

A better request would be:

"Hi, this is Ross. I was wondering if you'd like to go miniature golfing with me this Friday."

"I'd really like that! What time?"

"Is seven OK?"

"Sounds fine."

"Good, we'll go out for a pizza after and be home about eleven o'clock."

"That's perfect. I'm looking forward to it!"

"Me too."

He asked directly, and she was able to respond directly. Each told the other how glad they were that they would be going out. She knows what to wear, and he knows what he'll be spending. This happy beginning may lead to all sorts of happy tomorrows!

Challenge: Some people arrange to be together in situations that might not be called dates. He might offer to help with her English project. She might ask his opinion on a survey she's taking. What other creative ways might you find to get to know someone you like in a "nondate" situation?

Should Girls Ask the Guys?

Traditionally guys ask the girls for dates. Can it work the other way around? Opinion differs. Some say its OK for certain events. Others say its never right. Some guys are turned off when girls ask them out. Others don't mind.

Because girls often are more mature than guys their same age, they feel more confident about dating matters. This can make it easy for them to be too aggressive. If a girl is telephoning or asking a guy more than he is asking her, she's pushing too hard. If he's doing no leading, there's trouble.

Think: Do you think girls should ask guys out? What are the advantages and disadvantages?

Learn to Communicate

Rachel was thrilled that Ike had finally asked her out. But she ended up so worried that she would turn him off that she said little all evening. Ike thought he had bored Rachel, so he never asked her out again.

Warren, excited about impressing Hollie, agreed with everything she said. Hollie enjoyed Warren's attention but wondered if he had any opinions of his own. She knew little more about him after their date than before they went out.

Alyson talked about herself and her interests all during her date with Patrick. Patrick enjoyed her jovial spirit and freedom to share her ideas but couldn't get a word in edgewise. When she got home, Alyson wanted to kick herself for talking so much.

All three couples are concerned about making a good impression, and rightly so. First impressions often determine whether a couple will begin or continue a relationship. But these couples failed to communicate. Also called "talking" and "getting to know each other," communication is crucial to dating happiness.

The good news is that communication problems can be overcome! Communication skills improve with training and practice:

Tips for Talking

1. *Believe that what you have to say is interesting.* If Rachel had believed her thoughts were worth hearing, she would have talked more. Ike wanted to listen; she just didn't realize it.

2. *Don't do all of it.* No matter how fascinating Alyson was, Patrick needed to talk too. Dialogue (two people talking with one another) builds firmer relationships than monologue (one person talking to another). Alyson was so nervous that she couldn't enjoy listening.

3. *Ask questions.* Asking questions is a good way to express interest in your date and to draw her into conversation. Perhaps Ike or Hollie could have used these questions to show interest and encourage Rachel and Warren to talk: "What did you do this weekend?" "What did you think about the play?" "How did you feel about what the teacher said?" "Why do you think she reacted that way?"

4. *Begin with neutral topics.* Gradually progress to more important ideas and dreams. Rachel would feel comfortable talking about the weather, last night's ball game, or homework.

5. *Tell just enough detail.* People like enough detail to make the story interesting but not enough to bore them. When Patrick began yawning or looking distracted, Alyson could have asked him a question or gently changed the subject.

6. *Develop an easy-to-listen-to pace.* If you talk too fast, slow down. If you talk too slow, speed up. Though it may be clumsy at first for Alyson to decrease how much and how fast she talked, she'll gradually develop a natural pace.

Laws for Listening

1. *Pay attention.* Listen as though you'll be tested on the material! Warren remembered Hollie's details and noticed her feelings. He even

jotted down a few things she talked about after their date. He planned to ask her about them later.

2. *Be totally captivated by what the other says.* Refuse to doodle, look around, shuffle, or be otherwise distracted. Express your interest by looking into the person's eyes, turning toward her with your body, nodding as you understand, saying "uh-huh" and "oh!" at appropriate times. Patrick did this so well that Alyson couldn't stop talking!

3. *Repeat back.* From time to time, repeat in your own words what you think the other is saying. "It took that long! Did you think you'd ever finish?" asked Warren.

4. *Count to ten before you respond.* Alyson was so afraid of silence that she filled it with chatter. She decided to try this suggestion to keep from jumping in or monopolizing the conversation. Especially if your date is shy or quiet, a bit of silence gives him opportunity to speak.

5. *If you aren't sure, ask!* Ike and Rachel's relationship stopped because they failed to talk about what they thought was happening. This brief conversation might have given their relationship a future:

"Rachel, I hope I'm wrong, but I feel I'm boring you. You're not saying anything," said Ike.

"No I'm not bored! I just get quiet when I'm nervous, and I'm worried about your having a good time!" responded Rachel.

"Don't worry! I wouldn't have asked you out if I didn't think I'd have a good time with you. I want to hear what you have to say," assured Ike.

The two could then sigh with relief, have a good laugh, and move on to better conversation.

6. *Listen about as much as you talk.* Your date wants to know you as well as tell about himself. Warren listened so well that he didn't talk. Alyson talked so well that she didn't listen.

Challenge: Apply the talking and listening tips to your life.

Make Your Actions Match Your Words

You use more than your mouth and ears to communicate. For example:

Your *eyes* talk and listen by looking into your date's eyes, by expressing interest, and by glancing with admiration.

Your *hands* gesture what you say. Hands can demonstrate the size of the fish you caught better than your words.

Your *face* expresses emotion, compassion, or frustration. A smile can say, "I understand." A frown can say, "I'm sorry."

Your *shoulders* can say "I'm depressed" or "I'm delighted!" Notice people's shoulders at school. What do they say?

Your *eyebrows* can question, doubt, agree, expect, or show seriousness. What are your eyebrows saying right now?

When your words and body don't "say" the same thing, people tend to believe your body:

"I'm not mad!" said Greg.

"Then why are your shoulders tense, and why are you shouting?" responded Wendy.

At the same time, because body language can mean different things, words are necessary to tell the difference:

"You're really distracted. You seem to be ignoring what I say. What's bothering you?" asked Abby.

"I'm not upset at all," clarified Adam. *"I just didn't get any sleep this weekend."*

Challenge: Become conscious of what your whole body is saying and grow to be as honest as you can.

Keeping a Good Thing Going

Once you've found someone you like, you'll want to keep the good thing going. Chapters 4 and 5 detail several ways to do so.

4
Dates: Enjoy Them

How can you make your first date, and subsequent ones, unforgettable? Try these tips:

Plan your dates ahead of time. Rather than simply "doing something" together, decide what you will do and where you will go. (This chapter lists over fifty ideas.) Planning each date lets you and your date know what to expect. At first choose dates with plenty of activity. This eases the pressure to entertain and impress each other. As you get to know each other better, progress to less-structured dates and enjoy the planning as well as the date itself!

Choose events that encourage conversation. Talking is one of the best ways to get to know each other. Share what you liked and did not like about the play. Laugh about your mistakes in the game. Praise each other's work on the project. The best activities are ones you can talk about before, during, and after.

Learn to be yourself with each other. In your eagerness to impress, you probably fear saying or doing the wrong thing. But its not fair to you or your date to put on a show. You have impressed your date enough for him to ask you out. Now let him know you. Let him know that you really do like football, that you get nervous before big speeches, and that you like his eyes. Make it easier for your date to be himself by showing interest in him. Ask about what he likes and doesn't like, where he likes to go, his talents, fumbles, hobbies, favorite subjects, and more.

Avoid the overly sophisticated, overly casual. An activity you're comfortable doing will likely be fun for your date. Especially at first, fancy dates like the prom or extravagant restaurants create pressure to act and look perfect. You're nervous enough! Don't make it worse! Too casual can also create pressure. Watching TV at your house may be fine after you know each other better, but structure makes your first dates more relaxed.

Enjoy. The more relaxed you are, the smoother the date usually goes. Pray that God will help you relax. Then concentrate on your date. As you try to make your date comfortable, you'll forget about your own uneasiness.

Add variety. After you've dated awhile, its still wise to plan ahead, talk, and be yourself. But expand the types of things you do together. Go out in groups and alone; spend time with each other's friends and relatives; do homework and chores together. Remember: The greater variety of things you enjoy doing together, the more likely you will become, and stay, a happy couple.

Try More Than the "Dinner-and-a-Movie" Standard

Standard dates are "go out to eat" and "go to the movies." What do these teach you about each other?—what she likes to eat, how he behaves in the movie theater, the quality of his table manners, and how well she talks while eating.

Consider how much more you can learn when you vary your dates:

Go out with groups—Does he treat you the same or differently when other people are around? How comfortable are you with each other's friends? How does she act toward people who are different from her?

Cook a meal together—How well does he enjoy cooking and cleaning up? How do you make a humdrum task fun?

Attend Bible Study and church—What does he think about Bible study? How much does she participate? What ways can the two of you discover to apply the sermon to your lives?

Study—What study habits does he have? How important is school? How willing is she to help with your homework?

Grow a garden or work on a school project—How do the two of you enjoy a long-term project? How well do you cooperate?

Write love letters—How well do you put into words your feelings about each other? Can you state specific things you like about each other?

Play games or sports—How fairly does he play? Does she exercise good sportsmanship? How well does he lose?

Watch sports—How does she act in a public place? How well does she enjoy the game? How does he react to unfair calls?

Jog or exercise—How important is physical fitness to her?

Do chores—How much fun can you have working together? How willing is he to share the work load?

Read and talk about the Bible—How easy is it to talk about spiritual things? What questions does she have about God?

Share a picnic—How well can you talk in an unstructured setting? What outdoor games does he like to play? How does she like nature, bugs, and summer?

Go shopping—What taste does he have in clothes and other possessions? How easy is it for her to make decisions? How well does he budget money?

Explore a museum—How does he feel about history? What exhibits does she like best?

Take a child to the park—How does she relate to children? Can he have fun doing "childish" things?

Spend an evening with each other's parents—How does he like your parents? How do they like him? How does she get along with her own parents? How do you like her parents?

Visit an elderly friend or relative—How does he relate to old people? How does she feel about growing old?

Go to your favorite activity—How does he feel about your choice? If he doesn't like it, how willing is he to do it with you and learn to like it?

Here are fifty more ideas suggested by youth. What could you learn about each other while having fun these ways? Use these these as starter ideas to come up with fifty other possibilities.

Work a jigsaw puzzle	Play miniature golf
Go to the planetarium	Swim/boat/water ski

Make popcorn
Tour the city
Cut each other's hair

Choose and read a library book
Visit a shut-in
Volunteer in Bible school
Play racquet ball, tennis, Ping-Pong
Attend church activities

Take a long walk
Ride bicycles
Ski, ice skate, or play hockey
Shoot baskets
Watch each other's ballgames
Bowl
Play tackle football

Gather a group for food and fun
Attend Christian concert or speaker
Play croquet
Play computer games

Attend a play/opera
Find constellations
Make cookies
Look at baby pictures

Talk, talk, talk
Play Frisbee football
Teach a child to ride a bike
Ride horses

Tutor children together
Program a computer
Fish/hunt

Play golf, bowling, or tennis
Go jogging
Go to the zoo/circus
Tour an interesting city

Play card games
Play wiffle ball

Visit relatives
Tell each other what you appreciate
Clean each other's houses

Go to an amusement park

Attend a recital
Go to a car show/demolition derby
Go to the beach or lake
Notice the shapes of clouds
Attend a conservatory
Go to each other's houses

Think: Which of these cost less than five dollars? Choose twenty you are willing to try. If you tried them all, you could date almost a year without repeating the same date!

Express Love

Casual dates give you many opportunities to express love. After all, isn't loving what dating is all about?

Pause now and read God's definition of love in 1 Corinthians 13:4-7. How might you express love to your dates according to these guidelines? Here are some starter ideas:

—Encourage the other on an important test/game/event.

—Talk about feelings of jealousy until you can deal with them.

—Be excited when your date wins an award (even if you wanted it).

—Refuse to gossip about someone's trouble.

—Compliment each other at least once a day.

—Read and discuss the Bible.

—Refuse to criticize each other in front of someone else.

—Bear with each other's bad moods.

—Trust each other enough to give freedom.

—Refuse to be rude.

—Consider your date's feelings and opinions.

—Make decisions together.

—Solve problems rather than brood over them.

What else can you add to the list? (Notice that kissing and hugging are not on the list. These are only two of many ways to show love.)

Think: Romans 13:10 says, "If you love someone, you will never do him wrong." How well did you express love on your last date according to this verse? Talk with God about it. He understands and has the power to improve your love life.

Group Dates

Group dates have definite advantages which include:

• It's more comfortable to get to know someone in a group.

• Groups give you opportunity to discover who you want to date.

• You can usually group date younger than you can single date.

- Many group dates are less expensive.
- You don't have to be "asked out" to go on a group date.
- Groups can do things couples cannot do, like get a discount to certain places, play ball games, or fund a Christian concert.
- Group dates can be great practice for single dates.

Participate in group dates whenever you can. Even after you've been single dating for awhile, group dates can help you get to know your sweetheart better, help you avoid sexual temptation, and give you something interesting to do.

Think: Which of the fifty date ideas might be best with groups? Best as a couple?

Challenge: Make every experience with the opposite sex an opportunity to practice relationships. The more people you know and get along with, the better your relationship with THE person will be.

Avoid Dating Destroyers

Flexibility, patience, and acceptance are generally helpful when dating. But certain actions are clearly dangerous and should never be tolerated. If the person you are dating, or considering dating exhibits any of these, stop dating him or her, especially if the person doesn't change after you have tried these suggestions:

The Insensitive: You are a quality person. Everyone, including you, deserves respect. When you expect good treatment, you usually receive it. If your date says or does something rude, cruel, or violent, refuse to put up with it. Respond firmly but kindly, "Please don't do or say that again."

If the behavior continues, return home (carry money to call your parents or a friend). Refuse to date the person again.

The User: Everyone has met the user. The user dates to satisfy her own needs. She may need a date for the prom. Maybe she wants sex. Perhaps she's trying to make a former boyfriend jealous. Whatever the reason, the user dates you once or twice and then drops you. The user is often charming on the date but treats you rotten in other situations. Avoid the user completely.

The Impresser: The impresser is always on stage. He never shows a weakness, never admits a fear. Everything is together and cool. The impresser doesn't realize that the best impressions are made by genuine people who admit their weaknesses as well as strengths. If you find yourself with an impresser, assure him that he doesn't need to impress you. You like him already. If he refuses to be himself, move on to someone more secure.

The Threatener: "If you leave me, I'll kill myself." "If you don't stay with me, I'll come after you." The threatener tries to control his dates with threats. Force never strengthens a bond. The strongest dating relationships are built on trust, freedom, and openness. If your date refuses to grant these, refuse to see him again. You won't help him or yourself by staying with him. If you are in danger, tell an adult who can help.

The Critical: "Why do you act that way?" "You are so dumb!" "I can't believe you did that again!" Youth have enough trouble liking themselves without someone pointing out more faults! The one you love should be your greatest fan. If you find yourself constantly criticized by your date, break things off. Find someone who notices your good points more than your bad points.

Note: Sometimes youth stay with someone who treats them poorly because they believe they can get no one better. This is simply not true. If you respect yourself, others will too. You deserve happy relationships. God wants people to treat you lovingly. Love yourself enough and trust God enough to break up with someone who treats you poorly. There may be a period of loneliness before you meet someone else, but you will meet someone. Brief loneliness is better than a lifetime of suffering.

Challenge: Choose carefully the people you date and the groups you spend time with. Then have fun!

5
Closeness: How it Grows

"I'll know him when I see him. Our eyes will meet, and we'll realize instantly that we are right for each other. He'll be shy at first, but once he asks me out, things will develop perfectly. I can hardly wait!"

A storybook romance! Wouldn't it be wonderful? It might be except for one minor catch: The only place such romances happen is in the storybooks. Real closeness takes time, commitment, and work. There is no shortcut. There is a happy ending though: Real life romances are better!

Notice the Clues of Closeness

Clues that a close relationship is possible include:

Common Interests: The more alike you are, the more likely you will grow and stay close.

Genuineness: Willingness to be yourself, to share thoughts and feelings honestly is crucial to a close relationship.

Respect: Respect says, "I care about your feelings, your ideas, your accomplishments, and your future. I think your needs are as important as mine. I show my respect in words and actions."

Initiative: Close couples deliberately spend time getting to know each other. They call and invite each other to do things.

Mutuality: The best sweethearts share the work. No love can survive when one person does all the giving or all the taking.

Learn to Love

"I want to grow closer to Gary, but I don't know where to start. Everyone says if its 'right' it will come naturally."

It's true that many relationships develop naturally. But *naturally* doesn't mean "without effort." Closeness grows as both of you get to know each other and learn how to meet each other's needs—needs like appreciation, affection, acceptance, and encouragement. It takes time to learn what each other's actions mean, how to communicate, how to respond to each other's bad moods, how to cheer each other up, how to show you care.

This learning comes through three Ts: talking, time, and tolerance.

You and Gary must *talk* often and about everything. The more subjects you can talk about and the more thoroughly you talk about them, the better. True closeness means being able to share genuinely and to understand each other on every area of life. As your relationship progresses, open it to more and more topics:

How to be happy	Relationships with friends
What I want from you	What you want from me
Jobs/career I want	Male/female roles
The Bible	Physical expression of love
My insecurities	My strengths
Your insecurities	Your strengths
Sex	Money and how to spend it
School	Growing old
Dying	Living
How to settle arguments	Religious beliefs
Family: my current one	Family: my future one
What I like to do	What I don't like to do
What I worry about	What pleases me
What marriage is like	Whether you want kids
Church commitment	Whether to date others

Think: Are there any topics you avoid? These signal danger! Truly close couples can talk about everything.

Time brings ease in talking about difficult subjects. Time promotes understanding. Time grants willingness to work out problems. Time settles strong emotions and makes forgiveness easier. Time helps you become comfortable with each other. Time can demonstrate your areas of similarity and conflict to help you assess how right you are for each other.

Think: Can a dating couple spend too much time together? What problems might indicate too much time together?

Tolerance knows that everyone has irritating habits, everyone sins, and everyone is still learning how to love. Tolerance accepts the other person while gently encouraging him to grow.

Think: What is the difference between healthy acceptance and tolerating sin? Between being tolerant and being used?

Read On: Pages 37 and 51 detail actions you never want to tolerate.

Risk Going Deeper

"Since we all want closeness, why is it so hard?"

Cultivating closeness requires great risk. As you share thoughts and feelings, you risk rejection. This rejection is easy at a superficial level. Rita doesn't really care if someone agrees that the weather is nice. But when she says, *"This may sound dumb, but I want to be an astronaut."* she doesn't want to hear, *"Yep, that's dumb all right."*

When she risks sharing this important dream and her dream is criticized or rejected, she feels criticized or rejected.

To keep from experiencing the pain of rejection, many people refuse to talk about their thoughts and ideas. Their dreams are never criticized because they never share them. But they also never experience the joy of being accepted, encouraged, and loved. Only when you risk rejection can you find love.

Grow Close Relationships

When you find a person whom you want to risk knowing better, what steps can you take to grow your relationship?

Listen. Express your interest through listening. You cherish most those who want to hear what you say.

Understand. Rita wants to be an astronaut. You don't want to be one and don't even know what one does. How can you understand? Ask! "What interests you about aeronautics?" Be certain your questions communicate interest, not criticism.

Share. Reveal your own thoughts and ideas. Those who accept your surface ideas are good candidates for deeper talking.

Disagree. Agreeing with every thought and admiring every action seldom builds closeness. The happiest couples communicate disagreements openly but gently. They show their respect for each other's ideas by listening and trying to understand the other person's point of view. Hint: Point out at least one area of agreement with every disagreement, "I couldn't be an astronaut because I can't concentrate under pressure. But I certainly would love to see all those new places!"

Support. You need sweethearts who will believe in you, who won't think your ideas are dumb, who will be there when you fail, and who will rejoice when you succeed. Remind your date that you support what she does and thinks. Remember and ask about things that concern her: "Did you find out any more about the requirements for the astronaut program?"

Smile. Your smile makes people happy. Use it generously to show care, interest, pleasure, excitement, and love.

Laugh. Humor helps couples weather differences. Be quick to laugh at yourself and slow to laugh at your date. Refuse to use sarcasm. Sarcasm's purpose is to say something cruel under the guise of humor. Let your laughter make your sweetheart feel better, not worse.

Reassure. Even the most secure people occasionally feel that no one loves them, that they are incompetent and worthless. Daily reassurance of your love can help your sweetheart face the challenges of each day. Just knowing that one person cares makes other problems seem less severe. Renew your love daily.

Read On: How will living by Ephesians 4:15 and 4:29 grow closeness?

Recognize Your Assumptions

Many of the problems you encounter in relationships come because you act on false assumptions. Most of these are unspoken but followed diligently. Three of these problems are:

1. A couple may operate under different assumptions causing confusion and conflict:

His—*"If you like me, you'll date only me."*

Hers—*"If our love is meant to last, it will do so even when we see other people."*

2. One may assume a problem when none exists:

"She's not talking, so she must be mad." Her silence can also mean:

I'm comfortable enough with you to be quiet.

I'm thinking about what you said.

I'm worried.

I'm frustrated.

I don't know what to say.

I'm tired.

3. One may fulfill expectations the other does not have:

"Because he's pressuring me to have sex, he must plan to leave me if I don't."

Instead he might mean:

I'm testing you to see what kind of girl you are.

I want this, but I know we'll be happier if we wait.

I'll leave you if you do have sex with me.

Clarify Your Assumptions

The best cure for the confusion caused by silent assumptions is talking.

"But she might not agree with what I say!"

"What if we start talking about our relationship and I find that he likes me less than I like him. I'd be embarrassed!"

"I don't know how to put into words how I feel."

Nobody wants disagreement, embarrassment, and confusion. But as you risk these, you often find agreement, comfort, and understanding. In fact, avoiding talking causes pain of its own:

"Why won't you go to the concert? Don't you like me?" asked Hal.

"Of course I like you, I just don't care for that kind of music!" reassured Mary. *"Can we go to the other one instead?"*

Before talking, Hal assumed that Mary refused his offer because she did not like him. If they had not talked, he might never have asked her out again.

"How could you accept a date with Brad when you knew I liked him!" accused Ora.

"I like him too. I didn't do it to hurt you," answered Rachel.

Girls are famous for spotting the guy they like and spreading the word. That fellow is then off limits. Anyone who accepts a date with him is accused of not caring. Talking about this unreasonable restriction can save Ora and Rachel's friendship.

Will Going Together Help Us Grow Close?

Advantages of Dating One Person	Disadvantages of Dating One Person
Get to know each other well	Tend to take each other for granted
Security of having a date	Feel trapped or limited
Feel loved and accepted	Fear the other will break up
Feel safe	Can miss meeting someone better
Prestige of being attached	May promote possessivenes
Learn loyalty	Can get too serious, too soon
Learn to show affection	Temptation to go too far sexually
Can communicate well	May neglect other relationships

The main advantage of going steady is the opportunity to get to know one person really well. Seeing each other in a variety of situations and talking about every imaginable subject is crucial for predicting marital happiness.

The main disadvantage of going steady is that it limits contact with other people. It may keep you from discovering the person with whom you want to spend the rest of your life. Also you tend to neglect friends of both sexes when you concentrate on one sweetheart.

Recognize your reasons for wanting to date one person exclusively. After considering the advantages and disadvantages ask yourself:

Why do I want to date only this person?

What hesitation do I have about dating only this person?

Do I still have contact with other male and female friends? Does this relationship enhance or stifle my other friendships?

Does going together make it harder or easier to control our physical intimacy?

Does this relationship make me more of who I want to be or make me want to hide my true feelings and convictions?

As you decide whether to go steady, be good to yourself. Get plenty of advice from your friends and from adults you trust. Then be smart as you evaluate that advice.

Think: When is going steady a healthy covenant? When does it cause problems? How could not going steady help you grow closer?

Match with the Master

The only assumptions worth following are those which match the Christian's relationship with God. Evaluate your love relationships by God's definition of love in 1 Corinthians 13:4-7:

In a lasting love relationship both partners are:

Patient	Kind
Happy with the truth	Ones who never give up
Always faithful	Always hopeful

They refuse to be:

Jealous	Conceited	Proud	Rude
Selfish	Irritable	Happy with evil	

Ones who hold a grudge (keep a record of wrongs)

Ora felt *jealous, irritable,* and *selfish* when the guy she liked asked her best friend for a date. There is nothing wrong with experiencing these emotions. The wrong comes in letting them continue. As Ora recognizes these emotions, she can talk them over with God and let Him develop the *patience* and *hope* she needs. She can then trust God to guide her to a boyfriend when the time is right. Only with God's help can Ora be *kind* to Rachel and *happy with the truth* that Brad likes Rachel.

Think: How would God's way of loving enrich your romantic life?

It's Worth It!

"You get what you pay for."

It's true in relationships too. The more you are willing to put into a relationship, the more you will likely receive in return. Close relationships come when you invest yourself in people who are willing to invest in you. As with material purchases, sometimes you get a bad deal, but don't let that stop you from investing. The dividends are more than worth it.

6
Sex: God's Good Gift

"God created male and female and blessed them. He then said, 'be fruitful and multiply, but do not enjoy it. I created sex to bring babies, not pleasure.' In fact, you'll be more holy if you have no part of it.'"

You say you've not read these verses before? Isn't sex kind of nasty and only for those who are no longer pure?

Not at all! The Bible actually says: "The Lord God said, 'It isn't good for man to be alone; I will make a companion for him, a helper suited to his needs'. . . . [God] brought her to the man. 'This is it!' Adam exclaimed." (Gen. 2:18, 22-23, TLB).

Imagine Adam's feelings when he woke to see the first woman walking toward him! Some translate his response as "Wow!"

Adam recognized God's good gift. Genesis continues: "That is why a man leaves his father and mother and is united with his wife, and they become one. The man and the woman were both naked, but they were not embarrassed" (Gen. 2:24-25).

God realized that we would not enjoy being alone. So He created opposite sex persons to delight us and gave us the yearning for a love relationship with one of these persons. He created sex as a celebration of that love.

Think: The Bible uses the word *know* for sex. How does sex help us know our marriage partner in the fullest way? How would knowing our partner in other ways make sex more enjoyable?

Why So Much Negative About It?

If God gave sex to us, why does it receive such bad press?

1. *People haven't read the directions.* God, the Master Designer, knows just how to use sex. God's instructions are in the Bible. But too many people refuse to read or heed them. Rather than using sex to express love, they use it to prove adulthood, to gain power, to avoid talking, or to satisfy oneself. These misuses of sex are promoted effectively in movies, novels, and commercials. But these are not the Manufacturer's instructions. And like any product, if sex is not used the way it was designed to be used, it causes more problems than it solves.

2. *Instead of "have sex according to God's directions," we usually hear "don't have sex."* Because so many misuse sex, some think all sex is wrong. But, sex is great when expressed God's way.

Discover God's Guidelines

Just as incorrect information can destroy sex, accurate information can give you the sex life God intended.

Too often we see God's commands as lines that we'd better not cross. This makes us want to get away with crossing them! But God's commands are more like arrows that point us to happiness. Because God wants our happiness, we can trust Him.

God respects us and allows us to make our own decisions. That's why He gave us freedom. But He also wants us to be happy. So He explains the right choices through the Bible.

Some of God's arrows are:

1. Your body and sexuality are good.
2. Sex is to be expressed in the security of marriage.
3. Sex is an expression of love, not proof of it.

God created sex:

- to provide pleasure, fulfillment, and relaxation,
- to symbolize the total oneness of the marriage relationship,
- for procreation (creating babies).

The Bible is full of information about sex. Some samples are:

- At creation, God spoke of sex as a good gift (Gen. 1:27-28,31; 2:23-25).

- The Song of Solomon can be read as a delightful love song from a man to his bride. It describes the pleasures of physical love.
- Proverbs 5:18-21 and Hebrews 13:4 speak of the joys of married sex.
- Genesis 2:25 describes Adam and Eve's comfort with each other's bodies.
- First Corinthians 11:11-12 explains that a married man and woman grow to be interdependent. They blend every area of their lives.
- Romans 12:1-2 encourages us to learn sexual guidelines from God, not society.
- Exodus 20:14; Matthew 5:27-28; 19:4-9; and Mark 7:21-23 explain God's command to keep sex within marriage.
- First Corinthians 6:15-20 explains that we can glorify God through sex.
- Proverbs 6:26-29 and 1 Corinthians 6:15-18 explain the dangers of sex outside of marriage.

Why Limits?

"Certainly sex is wrong when used casually, but I don't see why its wrong to express ourselves physically in a love relationship. Why can't we show our love?"

Rather than viewing waiting as something restrictive, recognize it as preparation for something better.

How are these the same: wild horses, running water, and raging fire?

Wild horses look beautiful but fight when approached. Only when harnessed and tamed can they bring the joy, power, and pleasure they possess. Like untamed horses, when sex is used without God's love and guidance, it kicks.

When running water is guided by the faucet, it quenches thirst. Without boundaries it floods, destroys, and terrorizes. Like water guided by a faucet, when sex is released within marriage boundaries, it meets needs.

When fire is in the fireplace, it provides warmth, fuel, and power.

When it is totally free, it consumes everything in its path. Sex needs to stay within marriage to provide true warmth and nurture.

Sex is only one way to show love. Other ways can be just as much fun and will make married sex better. Think of at least twenty ways to express love for your sweetheart without sex. Here are some ideas:
—Smile at the right time.
—Talk about something important to you.
—Listen as the other talks about something important to him.
—Send a love note.
—Say, "I'm sorry."
—Cook the other's favorite food.
—Help the other with a chore (fun when done together!)
—Ask the other's feelings about death and other hard topics.
—Say what you appreciate about each other.
—Talk out disagreements.
—Study together so both can make a higher grade.
—Write a song about your love.

Challenge: Adultery (sex with someone else's spouse), fornication (sex before marriage), incest, rape, and homosexuality are forms of sex without limits. These distortions of sex received severe punishments in the Old Testament and continue to bring problems today. Avoid them!

Why Wait?

"I agree that sex with everyone you date wouldn't be good. But if we're in love and plan to get married, why wait?"

1. People are, by nature, very jealous. You want your sweetheart to love you alone. Knowing he shared sex with someone else takes away some of the pleasure. Even if you plan to marry, you may change your mind. Wait until the wedding day.

2. Sex too soon usually becomes sex too shallow. Refuse to diminish your sexual pleasure by participating in sex before you are married. Sex before marriage usually strains the fragile love bond rather than strengthens it. Waiting helps seal the bond.

3. Sex is an expression of love. The best love includes emotional,

intellectual, spiritual, and social intimacy as well as physical intimacy. Dating without sex provides you the opportunity to build this foundation.

4. Sex is best expressed in a secure relationship. Marriage vows promise this security. Also, relaxation makes sex best, and we are most likely to relax in our own homes with our own spouses.

5. Sex gets better with practice. Each person is unique. Marriage provides time for a couple to learn how to please each other sexually.

Think: Did you know that married couples need sexual control too? Situations such as illness, or one is out of town, mean refraining from sex within marriage.

How Do I Set Limits?

"Well, since sex before marriage is wrong, how far can we go without going too far? Everybody always says, 'Until you feel guilty,' but there has to be something more definite! What if I didn't feel guilty until I'd gone all the way?"

As you decide your limits, consider these questions:

What if other people knew? If you feel comfortable telling adult Christians what you're doing sexually, you're probably fine. If you aren't sure, talk it over with an adult Christian.

What if God knew? If Jesus were sitting next to you, would you feel comfortable doing as you are doing? First Corinthians 10:31 reminds us to do all for God's glory. Does your physical expression encourage growth in Christ and Christian living?

Is it loving? Are you focusing on being good to yourself and your partner? Or are you working toward "how much can I get?" First Corinthians 10:24 encourages you to seek your date's happiness.

Exact limits may be different for each person, but certain areas are clearly off limits. These bring feelings that can only be satisfied through sex. Reserve them for marriage:

Stay above the neck and below the knee.

No hands under clothes.

No touching breasts or genitals, even through clothes.

Realize that setting limits is not only how much but also how long.

Even kissing can get heavy when it continues for hours! Rather than spending your whole date parking, fill your time with other activities that will help you grow closer.

Challenge: Learn to show you care through kisses and hand holding. A simple touch at the right time can be as romantic as an hour of parking!

Talk About Your Limits

"How can I save sex until marriage without looking frigid or hurting my date's feelings?"

What is said at your school about people who have sex? They get a "reputation," right? Of course, people also make fun of those who've never had sex. *Virgin* isn't always said with admiration. Yet someone with a "reputation" is usually liked less that someone who is a virgin. Contrary to locker-room talk, sexual limits are respected. Many dates push sex hoping you'll refuse. Biblical convictions are not only right but also work!

You may find it hard to talk about limit setting. But its much harder to deal with the problems caused by becoming involved in sex. Even though its hard, talk about your physical love with your sweetheart. It will get easier as you talk more. Always communicate your care as firmly as your limits:

"How can we show our love in ways that please both God and us?"

"I think we need to stop here. What do you think?"

"I'm glad you care enough to talk about this with me."

If you haven't already talked or if things move further than you know is right, communicate gently but firmly:

—Simply back away.

—Say, "I'd rather not."

—Gently push hands to a safe area.

—Say, "I like you, but let's express our love in other ways."

—Start talking.

—Say, "Humor me, and stop here."

—Suggest going for a walk.

—Say, "You have wonderful hands, but that's not where they belong."

Ideally both of you will work on setting and keeping limits. But if your date doesn't, be sure you do.

Challenge: Find dates who respect you and share your convictions. There are plenty of them!

How Can I Keep Limits?

"I agree that sexual control is important. But even when I set my limits, its hard to stop. Is there any way to control something that seems more powerful than I am?"

No doubt about it: Sexual control is not easy. But God promises never to give us anything we can't handle (1 Cor. 10:13; Phil. 4:13). So the first step is to realize that in God's power, you have control over your sex life. Talk with God about your feelings and desires. He can help you deal with them. God wants enjoyment for you, not frustration!

These actions have worked for other youth:

Plan your dates ahead of time. Dead time often becomes "parking" time. Keep busy enough that there is little time for sexual frustration. Chapter 4 gives over fifty ideas for fun.

Stay away from sexually tempting situations like parking, drive-in movies, time alone at home, double dating with couples who park, and parties where sex is encouraged.

Avoid situations that have been tempting to you before.

Talk about it rather than do it. Wanting sex means that you are perfectly normal! Talking can ease some of the tension. Talk about how you can hardly wait to get married and how nice it will be. Thank your date for helping you wait. Then find a nonphysical way to show your love (see suggestions).

Ask God to continue to give you patience. Turn your eagerness into anticipation!

Remember: There's no such thing as "I couldn't stop." These words really mean, "I didn't want to stop" or "I didn't know how to stop."

Lines Dates Use

"All this sounds fine if you've dated for awhile. But what about the first date? What if she wants me to go too far?"

One of the most effective ways of resisting sexual involvement is to recognize commonly used lines and practice responding to them. Line users may or may not realize what they are doing. But you can always realize what you are doing.

A few of the more common lines are:

A. "If you love me, you'll let me."

B. "I know you want to."

C. "We won't know if we're compatible unless we try sex."

D. "Men want experienced women. Let me be your teacher."

E. "Let me make a real man out of you."

F. "We have birth control, so its OK."

G. "Don't you care?"

H. "We won't go all the way, just this far."

When a line is used, respond firmly but kindly. One creative answer that will work with all lines is: "No, thank you" or simply "No." If you want to elaborate, try these samples:

A. "If you love me, you won't make me." True love doesn't force itself on others. True love doesn't use "love" as a tool. True love knows that sex is not the only way to express love.

B. "Of course I want to. But there are too many problems with sex before marriage. I love you enough to wait." Wanting sex is normal. Harnessing it until marriage is the best way to enjoy it. Sex before marriage cheats you and your sweetheart.

C. "I'm certain we will fit together physically. I need to know if we match in other ways, like expressing love without pressure." Every male is physically compatible with every female. This person is either ignorant of male and female anatomy or thinks you are.

D. "I'd rather gain my experience with the person I marry." Sex is a customized relationship which each couple develops their own way. There's no experience necessary! Within marriage talking and loving practice makes perfect!

E. "Real men don't have to prove it with sex." "Let me make a real man out of you" is especially popular as a movie theme. It sounds real macho, but its actually real stupid.

F. "No birth control is foolproof. Besides avoiding pregnancy is not the only reason I'm waiting." In addition, one or more of these problems come with every premarital sex experience: venereal disease (many of which have no cure), emotional pain, loss of virginity, strained relationships, and feeling used.

G. "Yes I care, but I don't need to make love to you to prove it." The pitiful line, "Don't you care?" plays on your sympathy. You worry that you'll hurt feelings if you say no. But say it anyway.

H. "Those feelings are for marriage alone." Not going all the way wants the feelings without technically breaking the rules. "Just this far" is usually too far. Rather than reassure you, this line should alert you to danger.

Think: Why is sex equated with love? How is love more than sex? How can sex be a way to use people rather than love them?

Reasons Youth Participate in Sex

"*I didn't really mean to get this involved. I've been a Christian since I was young. Now I'm pregnant. What will my parents say? What will my church say?*" Even though reasons to keep sex in marriage are clear, Christians are among those who become pregnant outside of marriage, who contract venereal disease, and who lose self-respect. Why?

"*It's fun.*" Its hard to wait for something good. But waiting makes it better.

"*I didn't know how to stop.*" "Talk About Your Limits" and "How to Keep Limits" in this chapter suggest ways to stop.

"*I was afraid he'd think I was weird if I didn't.*" We want acceptance so badly that we'll give our bodies away. But sex usually drives· sweethearts away rather than attracts them.

"*I wanted love.*" Sex is likely to destroy young love.

"*I wanted a baby.*" Babies are often sweet, but they also cry for hours in the middle of the night, require twenty-four-hour care, demand more love than they give, and need both a father and a mother. *"I didn't think it would happen to me."* Hope is not birth control. The consequences of sex come to whomever participates.

But I've Already Participated

"I'm one of them. I really didn't think sex was any big deal. But now that I take God more seriously, I realize that sex before marriage isn't good. What should I do? Is it all over?"

No, it's not all over. You can't change the past, but you can change the future. God offers you forgiveness and a fresh start.

The main problem with sexual sin is that sexual mistakes cannot be taken back. A baby created by the union remains. Venereal disease must be treated. Lost respect and devalued self-esteem must be restored. The memories persist.

Because the consequences of sexual sin remain, it is obviously best to refrain from it. But if you have already had sex outside of marriage, ask for and accept God's forgiveness. Then cease your sexual activity. This may be difficult, but God and friends will help you. Work through the feelings, problems, and guilt by talking them over with God and a trusted adult Christian. You are a person of worth, and God loves you fully.

Read On: John 8:3-11 describes Jesus' forgiveness of and adivce to a woman who had sex with someone she was not married to.

How to Have a Super Sex Life

To develop your sexuality God's way:

1. Remember that God created sex. As its Creator, He knows best how to enjoy this good gift. Understand God's guidelines.

2. Love yourself. Realize and accept that you are God's masterpiece. When you love yourself as God intended, you will not permit others to use you, to sway you with false promises, or to confuse you. Your respect will be returned by those you date.

3. Learn all you can. Read Christian books on sex and sexuality.

Accurate knowledge prevents your being misled by those who claim to know more than you do.

4. Ask questions. When you're confused, want to know more, or need help, ask! Christian adults want to answer your questions and help you understand God's good gift.

5. Determine your limits ahead of time. The backseat of the car is no time or place to decide how far you should go. All sorts of excuses can sound perfectly logical there!

6. Stick to the limits you set. Limits are no good unless you keep them. Love yourself enough to limit your physical involvement now. Your marital sex life will profit!

7. Express genuine affection in appropriate ways. Physical affection is perfectly right when it is not designed to lead to intimate sexual activity or intercourse. Kisses and hugs are special in themselves. (They're romantic too!).

8. Touch in nonphysical ways. Physical affection is only one way to express love. Love grows best when other ways of touching are included. See "Why Limits?" in this chapter.

9. Anticipate! God's good gift of sex is something to look forward to. Prepare yourself for it by learning all you can, by practicing yourself for it by learning all you can, by practicing your relationship skills, and by harnessing your sexual feelings. Trust and follow God's leadership.

10. Pray. Though listed last, this is first in importance. God can give you the strength to understand His guidelines and to stick to your convictions about sex. He will also help you relax while you date and find the mate He knows will make you happiest.

> It puzzles me, Father,
>   this mixed blessing, my body,
>   that you have given me.
> Sometimes I don't understand my body.
>   At times I am its master;
> Sometimes it masters me.
> There are times when my body is my friend,
>   and then, before I know what has happened . . .

It becomes my enemy.
Since I can't always understand or
 govern my body, Father . . .
 and because there are times when I really
 don't like it . . .
 I give it back to you.
I accept you as Lord of my life,
 and that includes my body.
Show me what you intended for me
 when you made me
 and what you intend for me now.
 Give me discipline
 and respect for my body.
Help me to see my body,
 myself, through your eyes of love.
—Jeanie Miley, *Take a Look at Yourself*
 (Nashville: Convention Press, 1981), p. 25

7
No Dates? Don't Give Up Yet!

To Date or Not to Date?

"Why don't I have any dates? I guess nobody likes me."

Though "Nobody likes me" is the first thing you think about, it is the least likely reason you are not dating. Did you know:

—Some of the most attractive people sit home many Saturday nights?

—Many guys ask out their second choice because it would hurt too much to be rejected by their first choice?

—If you aren't dating today, you may be dating this time next year?

—Some of the people who dated the least in high school have the happiest marriages?

—You can grow your dating skills when you aren't dating?

As you explore the reasons you aren't dating, ask yourself these questions. Then prescribe the tips following each.

Are You Letting Your Interest Be Known?

Perhaps you aren't letting prospective sweethearts know that you want to date them. Of course, you won't want to flirt to attract attention simply to satisfy your own ego. But honest flirting can let someone know you like him.

Rx: 1. Flirt in positive ways by: smiling at the right time; arranging casual contacts, such as attending her ballgame; eating at the restaurant where he works; asking if he's going to be there; making eye contact; talking; complimenting; staring.

2. More direct methods suggested by youth include: calling each other on the phone; going to each other's house; walking her to class; asking for a date.

THINK: What other ways might you let someone know that you like him? What clues are others giving that may indicate their affection for you? How do you want to respond to these clues?

Are You Too Self-Sufficient?

Without meaning to, you may sometimes project that you don't need anyone else. You may never share a problem, ask a question, or talk about ideas. This "safe" position keeps you from being criticized, but it never lets anyone close.

Rx: 1. Risk sharing yourself. Talk about what is important to you. This encourages those who like you to grow close to you.

2. Tell your friends what you like about them, why you need them. This helps them be themselves with you.

Are You Too Desperate?

Do you want a sweetheart so badly that you talk about it constantly? Do you feel that you must be dating to be happy? Men tend to run from those who want to "catch" them. Also you open yourself to being used when you insist on having a date.

Rx: 1. Cultivate a more relaxed attitude toward dating. Get to know your dates as people, not as happiness makers.

2. Learn to enjoy the other pleasures of life: friendship, success, nature, food, and exercise. Ask God to help you enjoy all creation, not just the dating part.

Are You Focused on Yourself?

Happy dating requires such skills as interest, understanding, listening, talking, and cooperation. Concentrating on yourself keeps these from developing.

Rx: Learn to forget yourself long enough to focus on other people. When you show interest in others, your own problems seem less important and you find yourself becoming happy. To find JOY, spell it out:

> Jesus, first
> Others, second
> Yourself, third.

Are You Too Shy?

Shyness is a form of selfishness. You fear others won't like you, so you refuse to talk or participate. There's nothing wrong with being quiet, but shyness can cripple you.

Rx: Gradually open yourself up to new friends and new experiences by forcing yourself to participate. You won't feel comfortable at first, but bit by bit you will. A sample:

Week 1: Daily say hello to someone you've never talked to before.

Week 2: Attend a church or school event you've never tried.

Week 3: Return to the event you tried last week.

Week 4: Talk in a group.

Are You Spending Too Much Time Alone?

You certainly can't meet potential dates if you sit at home on Saturday nights!

Rx: Volunteer to participate in a ministry at your church. Join a club that matches your interests. Find opportunities to both lead and follow, to learn and teach. This enables you to meet people and discover what types you want to date.

Are You Too Anxious?

Sometimes even the most attractive and likable persons simply don't have dates. Maybe they haven't met the right person. Maybe people are shy about asking. Maybe its not the right time.

Rx: Wait. The waiting is hard but worth it. God has promised to fulfill your need for love (Ps. 37:4). He won't let you down!

Do You Like Yourself?

If you don't like yourself, others will find it hard to like you. Loving yourself the way God loves you is the best way to project a datable image.

Rx: Read "Me First" in Chapter 10. Then perform daily the "Attractiveness Exercises" in this chapter.

Find People Like Yourself

"But where can I find dates? The ones I like, don't like me, and the ones I don't like, like me!"

Let people know the real you. You'll more likely find someone compatible with you when you share your real feelings and opinions. Participate in the activities you most enjoy. Excel in your areas of greatest skill. Speak out on issues that are important to you. When you feel pressure to act or talk a certain way to get dates, remind yourself that you'll be happier with someone who likes the real you.

Hint: Your comfort in being yourself is usually contagious. You may free someone else to tell you her true feelings.

Go out in groups. Take advantage of group events at your church and school. Attending group activities can be a low-pressure way to meet people and decide if you want to date them.

Free yourself to try something new. Ice skating may not be popular at your school, but if you think you might like it, try it! Be on the lookout for interesting people who are there.

Hint: Don't make "date hunting" your main reason for participating in any activity. Enjoy what you're doing no matter who is there. Sweethearts tend to show up when you truly forget about looking for them.

Get to know someone who doesn't seem that interesting at first. You may envision a tall, dark, handsome stranger who instantly falls in love with you. But most romances happen more gradually. Your "Prince Charming" may look very ordinary.

Consider the people you already know. Don was just what she wanted in a boyfriend: handsome and tall. She felt important when she was seen with him, but neither could think of much to talk about. She felt more comfortable with Alan. He was her best male friend. When they were together, they never had enough time to say everything they wanted to say. They acted so silly together. She never would have acted that way on a date! Yes, she and Alan were great friends, but nothing romantic took place. In fact, he was the one she went to when she had a boyfriend problem. That's why she was surprised when several people mentioned what a cute couple they were. Date Alan? But we're best friends! And he's so short! The more she thought about it, the more she admitted that they might be right. Shouldn't a boyfriend be your closest friend in the world?

Refuse to date someone you don't like. Don't lower your standards or settle for someone who doesn't meet your needs. If you're already dating when "Right" comes along, she won't notice you and vice versa. Less than best is often worse than none at all.

Grow More Attractive

"I realize I'd have more dates if I were more attractive, but I don't think I can change my looks!"

You can't change the basics, but you can enhance them! The first step toward outer beauty is to develop a beautiful personality. As one sixteen-year-old explained, *"Her face and figure are beautiful, but she complains all the time. There's no way I'd ask her out."* A more attractive inner you always makes a more attractive outer you. Likewise, an ugly personality can disqualify any beauty you have.

How would you apply each of these truths to your life?

• Proverbs 15:13 says, "A joyful heart makes a cheerful face" (NASB).

• Proverbs 25:23 says, "A backbiting tongue, [brings] an angry countenance [facial expression]" (NASB).

• Isaiah 3:9 explains that "the expression of their faces bears witness against them" (NASB).

The second step is to admit that physical appearance does count. In fact, it is usually the first thing that attracts us to someone. Before you disqualify yourself, remember that beauty comes in several forms. God gave some of these forms to you.

Recognize and develop both your inner and outer beauty:

• Every day, before you leave your house, look in the mirror and find something attractive about yourself. It might be your delightful smile or the way your hair hangs just right. God created you and likes what He made! (Gen. 1:31; Ps. 139:14).

• As you continue looking in the mirror, think of your best personality quality. Think about Jesus calling you His friend (John 15:15). Ask Him to help you develop the qualities of a good friend and sweetheart.

• Put your faults in perspective. You may tend to magnify your faults and deny your good points. But Romans 12:3 encourages you to see yourself as you are. This means to refuse to ignore faults that need correcting, but it also means to refuse to constantly criticize yourself. Accept your good points as well as your bad points.

God knows all facets of your personality, including your sins and ugly qualities. Rather than rejecting you, He continues to love you. When a fault surfaces, He offers help (1 John 1:9-10). He might suggest that you tame your temper by counting to ten before reacting. Follow God's instructions to grow toward the perfect person He knows you can become (though you won't make it this side of heaven). Then love yourself God's way.

• Accept compliments. God created you very special. Compliments are one way people notice God's handiwork! You may reject compliments, thinking, "If he really knew me, he'd not compliment me like that!" Resist the urge to magnify your faults and deny your good points. When someone compliments you, receive and enjoy the compliment. Then thank God for giving you that quality!

• Choose clothes and a hairstyle that enhance your natural beauty. Highlight the features God has given you by choosing colors, styles, and shapes that bring out your best. This requires creativity, not extensive finances.

• Use your beauty God's way. Talk with God about the physical and personality characteristics He gave you. How do you think your special characteristics fit into God's plan? Think about what you did well this past week. Thank God for working through you. Ask Him what He wants you to do next. Ask God to reveal His dating plan for you and give you courage to follow it!

Think: How can friends help you grow your beauty?

Recognize Dating Pressures

"Every time I stop worrying about my date life, somebody asks me why I'm not dating. Why can't they quit pressuring me?"

Most people are trying to express interest in you. Others are worried that you'll never marry unless they "fix you up" with someone. No matter what their motivation, a creative answer can hint to them that you'd rather talk about another topic:

"I don't like to date one person steadily in the summer. There's so much to do!"

"Oh, I'm interested in several. I haven't narrowed it down."

After you've answered, remind yourself that God loves you and that He does have plans for your romantic life. Refuse to give in to the pressure. As a youth explains, *"Everyone expects us to date. Then we do it for the wrong reason. I know girls who stay with a rotten relationship just to have a boyfriend."*

Challenge: When you have the dating blues, realize that its OK to feel sad that everyone is going the prom but you. It's realistic to be upset after a breakup. Its normal to want a sweetheart. Let yourself be sad for awhile, but don't stay there. Talk out your feelings with Jesus and with trusted friends.

Read On: Hebrews 4:15-16 explains that Jesus understands and can help with our dating woes!

Practice Your Dating Skills While You're Not Dating

Life does not begin with the first date nor end with the breakup. While you wait or recover, grow your dating skills.

• Practice getting along with people. Dating is not a requirement for learning to love. The same relationship skills are used in friendship, dating, and marriage. Spend time with people of the same sex and the other sex, people who are older and younger, people you like and don't like. With these people you can improve your ability to relax, to be yourself, to share ideas, to solve problems, to understand, to listen, to love.

• Improve your conversation skills. Learn to ask questions that encourage people to talk, that make them comfortable. Practice sharing your ideas in ways that don't threaten others. Learn to listen to what people are really saying.

Read On: See Chapters 3 and 5 for conversation tips.

• Focus on the pleasures of life. Friendship, spiritual growth, laughter, nature, success, good grades, and art are a few of God's other special gifts. Learning to enjoy them while you aren't dating makes them more fun to share when you are.

• Understand people. Answer these and other questions about every person you encounter. Each person teaches you how to understand every other person:

"Why does he act the way he does?"

"What feelings are behind that action?"

"What would I do in the same situation?"

"What makes her disobey God even when she knows He is right?"

"What words and actions calm him down?"

Read On: The Bible book called Proverbs contains insightful truths about why people act the way they do. Read one chapter a day for a month.

Enjoy Your Dateless Nights

Too often you may aim toward an imaginary standard of dating perfection and make yourself miserable while you wait. Nobody has a date every Saturday night. Instead of moping, youth suggest you try one of these on your dateless nights:

Have a friend over	Read a book or magazine
Cook	Participate in a Bible study
Talk on the phone	Talk to your parents
Rearrange your room	Work on your car
Write a story	Wash the dog

Attend a ball game   Work on a hobby
Write in your journal   Go out with friends

In the Meantime Enjoy Life!

The best romances are made of persons who are not waiting to become cuter, more popular, or richer to be happy. They thank God for who they are, grow toward what He wants them to be, and find pleasure in everyday events. As a youth explains, *"A person has to be able to be happy when spending time alone before he can be happy with someone else."* To increase your happiness:

—Enjoy your current relationships. If dating is one of those, great! If not, enjoy your friends of both sexes.

—Notice the good. Rather than focusing on the one bad grade on your report card, notice the four good ones!

—Compliment people. As you look for ways to compliment people, you'll enjoy them more and more.

—Cooperate. Life never goes exactly the way we think it will. When situations frustrate you, discover ways to bring good out of them. Romans 8:28 explains that God works in everything for good (see RSV or GNB). What plan does He have for your situation and what does He want you to do about it?

—Appreciate the problems you don't have. Though you'd gladly trade your loneliness problems for a set of dating problems, enjoy not having such problems as too little time for friends, the pain of breaking up, getting too serious too soon, sexual temptations, spending money on dates, and limited freedom.

—Pray. God is the author of happiness. Ask Him to help you see the good in your present situation. Trust Him to help you find a sweetheart more wonderful than you can imagine.

—Worship. As you focus on God and His love for you, you can't help but feel warm and cozy inside. He cares so much. Depend on God; He alone is the source of love and happiness.

Read On: Your loneliness will not last forever. Psalm 126:5 promises, "Those who sow in tears shall reap with joyful shouting" (NASB).

8
Problems: Handle Them Positively

Problems are part of life. Every dating couple has them. You'll find happiness when you solve your problems as they come and don't let the bad times keep you from enjoying the good times.

Learning to settle your differences, to talk out your problems, and to fight fairly are crucial to happy love. But some problems cannot be solved. What is the difference between normal dating problems and problems that signal you aren't right for each other? Couples who dated and are now happily married suggest these characteristics of *normal* problems:

- Can be worked out through prayer and discussion
- Help you learn about and accept each other
- Help you find out what your date is really like
- Are simple differences of opinion and tastes
- Mean compromising on matters that aren't consequential
- Each listens to and wants to help the other

Normal dating problems can be resolved naturally by talking or with time. Dangerous problems insist on major changes, such as beliefs, values, and upbringing.

The couples suggest that the following characteristics signal *danger.* Either you aren't right for each other or one person needs to solve individual problems before continuing the relationship.

- Topics you dare not talk about or that elicit anger
- Repeated breaking up and getting back together
- Neglecting your other friends
- Jealousy and possessiveness

- Physical or mental harm
- Conflict of beliefs, goals, and values
- Physical affection substitutes for love
- One insists on his own way in all situations
- One uses destructive emotions, such as pouting and threats
- One avoids conflict by always agreeing with the other

Hint 1: When there's no apparent conflict, somebody is hiding something. Because problems always come out eventually, find the problems you're suppressing and work toward solving them!

Hint 2: If you can't solve little problems while dating, you won't be able to solve any problems when married.

Read On: If you feel you may have dangerous or unsolvable problems read chapter 11. Pages 38-39 list five of these.

Problem Prevention

The best way to solve problems is to prevent them. Second best is to solve them while they're small. COMMUNICATION, CONFRONTATION, CUTTING BACK, and CARE SHOWING help you do both.

Communication

Communication occurs when both of you understand what the other person says and feels. You won't always agree, but you realize why the other person feels and thinks as he does. You each feel free to be honest because you know the other will understand and care.

Communication includes talking, listening, pondering what your date has said, and praying for understanding. As you communicate, be genuine, use gentle but true words, and talk until you both understand. For detailed tips on communication see "Learn to Communicate" in Chapter 3; "Recognize Your Assumptions" and "Clarify Your Assumptions in Chapter 5.

Confrontation

Recognize problems when you see them coming, and don't be afraid to bring them up. Its easy to think that if you act like everything is OK it really will be. But problems are a fact of life, and its normal to have a few. The earlier you bring them up, the easier they are to solve. *Confrontation* simply means to bring up the problem. Rather than accusing or blaming each other, attack and solve the problem together: "We have a problem" is better than "You are the problem." Bringing up problems can be scary, but the greater closeness that results from solving them is worth it!

Cutting Back

You can fight dating problems by cutting back on the ones you cause. You can't control your date's behavior, but you can yours:

- Rather than being demanding, be understanding: *"You've got a big test coming; I don't mind changing our plans so you can study."*
- Rather than taking your moods out on your date, talk about them: *"I'm feeling grouchy today. Its nothing you did."*
- Rather than deceiving your date, be sincere: *"When I fear that you don't like me, I want to go out with somebody else to see if you get jealous. I guess its better to ask for reassurance."*
- Rather than brooding, tell your date when you're upset: *"I wish you hadn't embarrassed me like that. I meant for that to be private. What can I do to help you understand next time?"*

Care Showing

Knowing the other cares makes problems easier to solve and eliminates certain problems: jealousy and possessiveness would vanish if we knew the other cared no matter what. Cultivate security by assuring one another of your care often. Learn many ways to say and show: "I love you." Here are twenty to get you started.

1. I need you.
2. I miss you.
3. You're beautiful.
4. You make me happy.
5. I like the way you . . .
6. You teach me so much.
7. I love looking at you.
8. I'm blessed to have you.

9. You have such good ideas.
10. I'm proud to be with you.
11. You do such a good job of . . .
12. Talking to you makes my day.
13. I feel comfortable around you.
14. You motivate me to live for God.
15. You make my life so interesting.
16. You're more fun than anyone I know.
17. I'm a better person because of you.
18. I chose you, and I'd choose you again.
19. Even the dull things are fun when you're around.
20. Let's work this out rather than letting it divide us.

Read On: See pages 37 and 51 for ways to show your love.

When I Don't Agree

Disagreements come to every couple. Handling them positively prevents unnecessary breakups. Many divorces occur simply because people don't know how to conquer their conflicts.

When you're upset with someone's words or actions, what do you tend to do/say?

A. "You're crazy! I can't believe you'd say/think/do that!"
B. Refuse to talk with the person again.
C. "What makes you say that?"
D. "What about . . ."
E. "Can we come to some sort of compromise?"
F. "I don't agree, but I understand why you feel that way."

A. This response puts both of you on the defensive. He now feels he must defend his viewpoint even if he knows he was wrong. You feel obligated to prove him wrong even when you start to understand him. Winning, rather than understanding, becomes the goal.

B. Based on the myth, "True sweethearts never disagree," this response cuts off anyone with differing viewpoints. The main problem with this response is that you run out of sweethearts. Everyone disagrees with everyone else at least once.

C. Understanding goes further in resolving differences than accusation. By sensitively asking questions you discover reasons for the other person's action. Perhaps anger, a bad past experience, teasing, or thoughtlessness was the reason for the remark.

D. Words like this encourage your friend to explore his own thoughts. If he is wrong, he'll more likely accept it if he discovers it himself. In an atmosphere of acceptance and understanding, you can explore disagreements together.

E. Disagreements can usually be solved through cooperation. For example, if you each prefer a different restaurant, go to neither and find a third that you both like. Or try both!

F. Often called "Agree to Disagree," this statement assures your friend continuing care.

Important!—Some disagreements signal danger. Matters of Christian truth and morality are absolutes. In these cases, use the Bible to guide the person to truth.

It's Not Easy

"Every time we have a problem I find myself either clamming up or yelling. I can't seem to talk calmly."

Consider the models you have for problem solving. Did the people you know solve problems by ignoring them or shouting about them? You unconsciously imitate them. Learn some new methods. For example, when the next problem comes up, think about what you want to say before you say it. You may even want to make a list so that what you say is what you mean. Then tell your date you want to talk about a problem. Explain that to keep from yelling or clamming up, you've written down your ideas. Read the list or let her read it. Ask her what she thinks the two of you could do about the problem. Then work together toward a solution.

Solving problems is never easy. Like any skill, you'll improve with practice, and you'll do better when someone works with you. Let solving problems strengthen rather than divide.

Read On: See Chapters 3, 4, and 5 of *Friends: Finding and Keeping Them* (Broadman Press, 1985) for more detailed communication and problem-solving strategies.

Challenge: Choose dates who will solve problems with you.

And Now Some Real Problems

These actual dating problems are followed by possible solutions. What else do you think would work? Which of the solutions apply to a problem you are facing?

He Likes Me: I Don't Like Him

"He asked me out, and I don't really want to go. But I don't want to hurt his feelings. I guess it won't hurt to go out with him just once for a friendly date."

This is a tough problem. But, yes, it may hurt to go out with him just once. Accepting a date usually indicates attraction. Unless both of you understand that it is a friendly date (and some dates are), you should not accept a date with someone you don't like. Put yourself in his shoes: If a guy you liked asked you out, you might think he thought you were more than just a friend. One date would give you hope for more. And even though it would be disappointing, it might hurt less if he never asked you out. Similarly, it may hurt this fellow to say "No, thank you," but it might hurt less than leading him on.

Green with Jealousy

"Julie and I aren't on the best terms lately. You see, she's dating another guy. I'm dating other people too, so my feelings aren't really fair, but I can't help being jealous."

Jealousy is a natural emotion, but it can destroy you if you don't control it. Jealousy comes because you doubt that the other person cares for you. You fear that the same qualities that attracted you to Julie will attract other guys. And they might. But hanging on tight doesn't guarantee that she will stay. True love grows only with freedom. Just as you want freedom, Julie needs it too. No matter how many people you date, if Julie is the one, you'll go back to her. It works the same way for her. Just imagine that Julie dated everyone she was interested in and still found you superior! Then imagine how you would feel if you knew Julie was still wondering about someone else when she married you. Dating around can confirm your relationship or demonstrate that other people are better for both of you.

Talk about your feelings of jealousy with Julie. Explain that though its hard for you to give it, you want her to have freedom. Pray that God will work in both your lives.

Will Love take God's Place?

"I've been talking to a strong Christian who says God wants all of me. Does that mean getting married would make my love and faith in Christ disappear? How does my relationship with Dale go with God?"

No, getting married would not make your faith in God disappear. God does want all of you, but what that means is that He wants to guide everything you do, not take everything away. God wants to guide how you date and who you marry. Then He wants to help your marriage become the happiest marriage ever. A Christian's marriage has been called a "holy triangle": Husband—God—Wife.

Your relationship with God affects how you treat your husband, and your husband's relationship with God affects how he treats you. The way you treat each other will enhance or distract from your faith. Being close to God brings a closer husband-wife relationship. Loving Dale can demonstrate your love for God: Because you love God, you'll will notice the best in Dale and gently encourage him to grow. You'll love him the way God does.

What Can I Say?

"Ben and I have been dating about four weeks. I am crazy about him, and I think he likes me too. We have a great time when we're doing something like miniature golf. Our problem is that we can't think of anything to talk about."

Even if both of you tend to be shy, you must learn to talk to each other. To begin with, talk about what you're doing—the golf game: *"Which hole did you like the best?"* *"I was really impressed when you . . ."* *"Next time I'd like to . . ."*

Then talk about the events of the week: *"How did your test go?"* *"What did your friend say about your job?"*

Then gradually introduce topics that are more personal: *"Someday I want to . . .";* *"My parents help me when . . . but they bug me when . . ."*

And finally, talk about your relationship: *"I appreciate you when . . .";* *"It's so fun when we . . .";* *"I wonder if you like me when . . .";* *"I get irritated when . . .";* *"I hope we'll . . ."*

Talking is essential to full happiness, and practice makes perfect! See Chapter 3 for tips on talking and listening.

The Company We Keep

"I started liking this guy who's real cute. He and his friends drink, but he never does it around me. He's nice to me and treats me well. I'm a little worried because I wonder if its OK to date someone whose friends drink. He seems like he really likes me though."

You become like those you spend the most time with. Though you may feel strong, 1 Corinthians 15:33 explains, "Bad companions ruin good character." Eventually your sweetheart will let down his guard and return to the recreations of his friends. By then you may want to go with him. Your smartest choice is to find a sweetheart who has qualities you want to imitate because you'll do so without realizing it.

9
Parents: An Asset Worth Considering

"Dealing with dating problems is a big job. I can use all the help I can get!"

Contrary to popular opinion, parents can be one source of help. They dated, fell in love, and felt the feelings you feel. Many would be glad to share their successes and failures. Work toward seeing your dating as a team effort:

"My family stands behind me"
rather than
"Me vs. my parents."

How Can They Help?

Following each way parents can help is one or more pitfalls. When you fall into the pits, work together to crawl out.

Help 1—*Parents can listen.* He finally asked you out, and you can hardly wait to tell someone!—or—You're upset and need an understanding ear. Most parents want to hear both your happy and frustrating experiences. When you volunteer to tell them before they ask, you feel less nagged, and they lecture less.

Pitfall: Some parents interrupt with comment or advice before you tell the whole story. Crawl out of this pit by gently saying, *"Please just listen to me. I need to talk it out."* Notice and appreciate when they listen to you.

Help 2—*Parents can model love.* Many parents have nurtured their love over the years. Even more in love than when they first married, they cherish being together and make adventures out of the mundane tasks of life. Notice the way your dad grins at your mom, the way she teases him, the phone calls just to say "I love you" and the way they comfort each other.

Pitfall: Some parents have let their love grow weak. They tolerate rather than enjoy each other. Notice what you do and don't want to imitate about your parents' love.

Help 3—*Parents can teach you how to act on a date.* As one sixteen-year-old explains, *"At first I was embarrassed when my dad told me how to impress a girl and nice places to go, but then I didn't mind. Sometimes Dad pushes too hard, but I just tell him that it bugs me. Eventually he lets me make up my own mind."*

Pitfall: Help may come across as a command rather than a suggestion. This can stem from parents' not knowing how to share their ideas or your unwillingness to listen. Much depends on how easily you and your parents talk about other subjects. The more subjects you can talk about, the easier it is to take advice.

Crawl out of this pit by practicing talking about all sorts of topics with your parents. Start with neutral ones like the weather. Then gradually ask for advice on other topics. Finally ask for dating advice.

Help 4—*Parents can be sensitive.* Parents understand what you're going through and can allow you freedom to come to them when you're ready. *"My mom's pretty good about leaving me alone,"* shared one youth. *"She gently asks, 'What's wrong?' but doesn't push. I'm more likely to go to her then."*

Pitfall A: Sometimes parents seem uncaring. Actually they're busy or preoccupied with their own problems. Just as your quietness doesn't always mean you're hiding something, their quietness doesn't always mean disapproval. Discover their reason by watching, asking, and trying to understand.

Pitfall B: Some parents push too hard. Their eagerness to help comes across as nosiness rather than interest. Crawl out of this pit by realizing that pushy advice usually means they're worried about you. Exchange a little talk for a little privacy.

Help 5—*Parents can be a source of comfort.* When your sweetheart has dumped you, your parents can sympathize, relate a time it happened to them, and help you find something to do.

Pitfall A: Some parents find it so hard to see their child hurting that they withdraw rather than help. Sometimes they "explain away" the problem with phrases like, "He wasn't good enough for you anyway." Crawl out of this pit by asking that your parents recognize the problem rather than ignore it. Assure them that you can handle the hurt.

Pitfall B: Occasionally you may have to find someone else who can sympathize. If you aren't going to talk with your parents, let them know why you're quiet, *"I'm feeling really down tonight. Please don't take it personally if I don't say much."*

Help 6—*Parents can help you solve your problem.* They can help you think through your dating problem and work toward a solution: *"Why do you think she's acting that way?"* *"What have you tried?"* *"Which of Jesus' teaching can help you handle this situation?"*

Pitfall A: Sometimes parents ask questions in an accusing tone. Try to ignore the tone and listen for ways the questions could help you solve your problem.

Pitfall B: You may feel the questions are an invasion of your privacy. As hard as it is, try to hear and trust your parents. Though they sometimes express it awkwardly, parents usually love you more than anyone else on earth.

Help 7—*Parents can give advice.* Sometimes you need more than questions. You need ideas. Ask your parents: *"What would you do in this situation?"* *"What do you think my options are?"*

Pitfall A: Some parents give advice as an ultimatim. They expect you to do as they say rather than simply to consider their ideas. Explain your need to decide for yourself. Ask for more than one set of advice, so you have some choice.

Pitfall B: It can be hard to listen to your parents' advice. Crawl out of this pit by realizing that it's probably the source of the advice, not the advice itself that bothers you. Ask God to help you swallow your pride and listen, even when the advice seems critical or controlling. Then make your own wise decision.

Help 8—*Parents can be an excuse.* Sometimes it's easier to say, *"My mom won't let me,"* than, *"I really don't want to."* Most parents would gladly agree to be the bad guy. Meredith asks her mom to wait five minutes after dropping her off at parties. Meredith then enters and checks out the party. If no one is there who interests her or if there is drinking or drugs, she quietly exists and meets her mom a block away.

Pitfall: You need to develop your own ability to say no and to stand up for your beliefs. Gradually work toward this while leaning on your parents for needed strength.

Help 9—*Parents can get to know your sweetheart.* When parents spend time with your sweetheart, they tend to trust him more and understand better how your relationship is going.

Pitfall: You usually feel nervous when first meeting each other's family. Climb out of this pit by reminding yourself that the better you know her family and the better she knows yours, the better chance you have for success. If your relationship gets serious, her family becomes your family.

Help 10—*Parents can give you practice solving fights.* Anytime two people are together, potential for disagreements exists. Solving the disagreements you have with your parents tones up your skills for solving romance squabbles. Communication works similarly no matter whom you are talking to.

Pitfall A: It's hard to solve problems with your parents. Begin by finding something you can agree on. A sixteen-year-old advises, *"There's no way you can be totally different. Listen to their view and try to compromise yours with theirs. If you look carefully, you'll find some idea of theirs that matches yours."*

Pitfall B: Parent problems seem more stubborn than romance problems. Some parents don't do their part. Some parents don't want to communicate. You can't make them understand you, but you can understand them. Usually your efforts result in your parents trying harder. But if they don't, it's not your fault. Just do all you can and pray that they will become open to you.

Note 1: Nobody's parents help perfectly. Most will excel in some ways and need practice with others. You can teach each other. As one parent said, "I've never been the parent of a dating fifteen-year-old before. Please bear with me as we learn together!"

Note 2: Some parents are not available, may not know how to help, or may not care. Perhaps no one ever taught them how. Realize that their inability to care is not your fault. When your parents cannot help, find other adults who can. In the meantime, keep trying to communicate with your parents.

What If They Don't Approve?

"Why do my parents make such a big deal about not liking my sweetheart? We're not getting married or anything! We simply enjoy being together. It's my life, and no one can tell me what to do!"

It's true. No one can tell you what to do, how to feel, and whom to like. Only you can make these decisions. This is both a privilege and an enormous responsibility. Every person you date, even if you go out only a few times, affects your present and future happiness. Because no one else can do it for you, take your date life seriously.

Parents make a big deal out of whom you date because they know dating is a big deal. Though they won't always say it in these words, one or more of these is behind their concern:

"Your date is a bad influence on you." You are influenced, for bad or for good, by everyone you date. A negative influence causes you to hesitate to express your beliefs and ideas. A positive influence frees you to say and do your beliefs. When your parents express concern, consider what they are saying and why they're saying it: Your parents may be right. They may be wrong. Or they may be picky—"No one's good enough for my son!"

"My baby's growing up." Many parents find it difficult to give their children independence. As a baby you depended on them for everything. Now you need them to set you free, to guide you rather than do for you. This role is foreign to some parents.

"You might marry him!" The one you marry will be someone you have dated first. Many people develop a love relationship before they stop to evaluate whether the person is the one they want to spend their lives with. Then they refuse to evaluate. *"I love him so it must be*

right." Parents know that when a relationship reaches this point there is little they can do. So they react in the earlier stages, hoping to avoid problems.

"*Don't do what I did.*" Your parents may have an unhappy marriage. They don't want you to experience the same misery. Parents know that marriage isn't all romance and fun. It includes hard work and cooperation. They want you to have a marriage that is happy from beginning to end:

Nancy had married at fifteen. When her daughter Lesley turned fifteen, Nancy clamped down. Nancy remembered how hard those early years were, how trapped she felt with tiny children when her friends were in college. She did not want Lesley to go through the same problems. Had Lesley known this, she would have understood her mother's sudden strictness.

"*You don't respect me!*" When you choose someone different than your parents would choose, they may see your choice as lack of respect. Some youth deliberately choose dates their parents don't like to defy them. Others simply have different tastes in sweethearts. Notice which is happening in your situation.

Talking It Over

"*Whenever we talk about who I date, my parents become angry. What do they have against me? I think I'll just drop the subject!*"

Conflict over whom to date is heavily charged with emotion. Because you feel so strongly that you are right and your parents feel so strongly that they are right, neither stops to think or listen. Difficulty talking about dating means that the subject is important, not that your parents hate you. Strong feelings on both sides indicate the need to try harder, not to back off.

1. *Realize that you are your parents' first concern.* Their emotion comes because they care, not because they don't. This is a crazy way to show love, but it's the only way some parents know.

2. *Evaluate your emotions.* Why do you like your sweetheart so much? What positive qualities does he possess? How might he be hurting you? Do you cling more tightly to him because of your

parents' resistance? Don't let conflict with parents drive you close to someone you don't really want.

3. *Count to ten before you speak (or yell!).* Maintain control of your emotions even if your parents don't.

4. *Listen.* What are your parents trying to say, and why are they saying it? Ask for clarification. When you listen to them, you earn the right to be heard.

5. *Communicate your views clearly and gently.* When your parents discourage you from dating Paula, share specifically what you like about her. Explain that she's quiet around them because she is shy, not because she is hiding something.

When They Still Don't Approve

You've talked and prayed and waited and hoped, but you and your parents still disagree. They forbid you to see him. What do you do?

Step one is to realize that the situation is not easy for anyone—you, your parents, or your sweetheart.

Second, take one more look at the relationship. Where are the problems: Are your parents mistaken? Do they see the relationship differently than it is? Or is there some truth in what they're saying? Is your sweetheart treating you poorly in some way? Are your friendships suffering because of him? Is he discouraging your commitment to God? Are you settling for less than the best because of pride or desire for a boyfriend now?

Third, study some truths about parents and dating:

A. Parents and dating are both important. Life is happiest when they can work together.

B. The best sweethearts are willing to get to know your family as well as you.

C. It is dangerous to hide a relationship from parents.

D. Parents can notice how a date affects you before you do.

E. Sometimes parents are right.

F. Sometimes parents are wrong.

Finally, work toward a solution. Pray for openness to God's ideas. List every possible solution, even those you would never try. Then, together with your parents, if possible, choose and work toward the best solution.

Possibilities include:

• Request that for one month you be allowed to invite him to your home rather than go out together. This allows your parents to get to know him and maybe trust him more.

• List what you do like and don't like about him. Ask your parents do the same. Compare and discuss lists.

• Agree not to date him for one month. Keep busy with friends and maybe other dates. When the month is over, evaluate how you feel about him. Ask your parents to listen to your feelings. Listen to their ideas. Decide what to do the next month.

• Ask your friends what they think about him. They notice how he influences you too. Rather than using them to build up ammunition against your parents, request that they be honest.

• Ask your parents to tell you (or write down if you find it hard to talk together) why they want you to stop dating him. Think about their reasons for a week before discussing them.

• Swallow your pride and do what is best for you.

Read On: Ultimately you'll want to follow God's advice. As Proverbs 2:1-12 explains, when you learn from God, He'll show you what to do and bring you pleasure.

Parents Are People Too

Each parent is a unique and special person. Becoming an adult does not grant all the answers or fix all problems. Parents are adults who are still trying to find answers to their questions. Give them the same understanding you crave from them.

Get to know your parents as people and as friends. Day by day, work toward making your relationship with your parents something you want to last a lifetime. Because it will!

10
Love: Have You Found It?

Couples who have been happily married several years say that they knew they were in love when:

"I never could do anything without wanting to tell him about it. I didn't want to go through the rest of my life without him. He was (and is) the only person with whom I could fully be myself. He brings out the best in me. I continually grow to be a better person because of him."

"We were as comfortable as a couple as we were as individuals. We worked together well."

"I never got enough of him. It seemed like there was always more to learn about each other. Our relationship had an anticipation which I'd never experienced with another man."

"Her Christian character, commitment, and goals were similar to mine. She was supportive, sensitive, and kind. We had mutual trust. My mind, emotions, and spirit all said yes!"

"He fit every qualification I had prayed for in a husband. Before I met him, I thought I had found the person I would marry. But it was an artificial relationship—we had to work too hard at it. With the person who is now my husband, things happened more naturally. He accepted me and encouraged me in all situations."

"Just thinking I was in love wasn't enough. I had to find someone who could enrich, enhance, and fulfill my life."

"I realized that he completed my personality—he had qualities I didn't have; he was strong where I was weak. I couldn't imagine living without him; he was too important to my well-being. I believe we are more of what we're intended to be by God when we grow close to the one we love."

How to Find True Love

Married couples who are still very much in love and who range in age from twenty-three to sixty-seven suggest these ways to find life-long love:

• *"Learn to have fun with the other sex. Seek friendships, not lovers. This way, when the one comes along, you're free to feel the difference and will have friends to help you."*

• *"Pray for direction from God on whom to date."*

• *"Find somebody you can really get to know, whom you're really comfortable with. You'll build relationships at many different levels and marriage is the deepest one."*

• *"Risk some confrontations when you don't agree. Everyone disagrees, and you can't find love without talking problems out."*

• *"Keep the relationship as friends before falling in love."*

• *"Be selective, and take your time getting to know dates."*

• *"Insist on communicating about inner feelings and personal philosophies on every subject. Spend plenty of time together."*

• *"Select someone with whom you have a lot in common. Be sure she possesses the qualities and traits you want to live with for the rest of your life."*

• *"Have fun! Don't always be thinking 'Is this the one?' Relax and get to know each other rather than worrying about getting serious."*

• *"Seek someone with a similar background and upbringing. This saves alot of discussion, fights, and adjustment."*

• *"Don't get serious about someone expecting to change her after marriage. If she doesn't change before you marry, she isn't likely to change after marriage."*

• *"If your sweetheart doesn't become a Christian before you marry, he probably won't after you marry. Its best to date someone who is already a committed Christian."*

• *"Girls, don't let your dates learn that you are afraid to be an 'old maid.' If they think you're after a husband, they run!"*

• *"Find someone who encourages you in your Christian faith. Ask yourself: What have you done for God as a result of your sweetheart's influence? What have you hidden or hesitated to do to please your sweetheart? Be sure there's more of the first!"*

Read On: Samson had everything going for him but let his love for beautiful women bring him problems and death (Judg. 14—16). Love is meant to enhance your strength, not destroy it!

Is It Love or Infatuation?

Youth listed these differences between infatuation and love:

LOVE	INFATUATION
Is caring and giving	Is lustful and wanting
Is real	Is in love with love
Knows the other well	Is just getting acquainted
Sees the other's faults	Sees the other as perfect
Respects and trusts	Is jealous and possessive
Is honest	Concerned about impressing
Wants to grow	Resists change or adjustment
Emotional, social, spiritual	Mainly emotional
Learns from other couples	Refuses to consider advice

Because most infatuation doesn't last, many people call it *fake.* A better label is *temporary.* "Not forever" does not mean "not important." Infatuation is very real and can teach you about love. You learn how to show your love through actions and words. As you nurture your relationship, the powerful infatuation feelings either grow into true love or fade away.

When you find yourself liking someone, enjoy it. Take it slow and treat your partner well. Refuse to make permanent decisions (engagement, marriage, or physical involvement) based on these potentially temporary feelings. Infatuation feels strong, but someone usually gets hurt when promises are based on it. Give your feelings time to grow. If it's true love, it will last.

If and when the feelings cease, be honest (see Chapter 11 for tips). Assure the other person of your care and appreciation as you talk about the end of your romance.

Think: Several experiences with "puppy love" or infatuation can teach you what kind of person you want to marry. What is the difference between learning from and using someone?

Challenge: When people tell you you aren't in love, you feel pressured to prove that you are. This may cause you to force a relationship that you don't really want. Recognize and refuse to give in to this pressure.

Separate Fact from Fiction

Fiction 1: You just know when you are in love.

Fact: Though some people seem to "just know," most struggle with deciding if its love. The butterflies may mean love, or they may mean your lunch does not agree with you. Give yourself time, ask yourself many questions (such as these following), and ask advice from people who know you well. Taking time won't threaten your love; it will strengthen it. Finally, based on everything you understand, decide whether you are willing to commit yourself to that person. Ultimately love is a decision: You decide to continue your love, no matter what.

Fiction 2: Love is a feeling.

Fact: Mutual romance is an exciting beginning to any relationship. But to keep that feeling, a couple must commit themselves to nurture their love. Love is more an action than a feeling. We decide to love no matter how we feel: We stay kind even when we're in a grouchy mood; we listen even when we're tired. True love models itself after Jesus' love.

Fiction 3: If I were in love, I would be happy.

Fact: Unless you are already happy, love will not keep you happy for long. The same problems that bothered you before will resurface. If you fight with your parents now, you'll fight with them after marriage. Love makes many problems easier to handle, but it doesn't erase them. Refuse to use love as an escape. Seek happiness and solve problems through your relationship with Christ. Then when romance comes along, you'll enjoy it more.

Am I in Love?

Deciding if you are in love is one of the hardest things you'll ever do. Strong emotions make it difficult to separate feeling from fact. Its hard to tell the real thing. But ask yourself the following questions.

1. Does this person bring out the best in me? True love brings out more of your good qualities than your bad. It frees you to grow your way, rather than pressuring you to conform to another way. How have you changed since you've been dating? Ask your friends and trusted adults to help you discern this person's influence on you. If it's positive, you may have found love.

2. Do we share the same beliefs and goals? True love does not compete with your convictions; it makes them stronger. The closest couples agree in their understanding of God and encourage each other to live those beliefs. True love finds it easy to talk about God and to get to know Him better. If the two of you avoid talking about religion, you haven't found love.

3. Do we know each other? The longer you've dated, the less chance you have to be surprised after marriage. We've all heard stories of waking up to a different person after the honeymoon. Be yourself, encourage your date to be herself, and share experiences spread over a long period of time. Notice each other's strong and weak qualities. Those in love know each other and like what they know. You'll never like everything, but the one you marry should score at least 90 percent!

4. Is school/work going well? True love motivates you to do better in every area of life. When you are happily in love, you'll make better grades, you'll do better at work, you'll get along better with teachers and bosses, and you'll be more excited about reaching your goals. If you find yourself preoccupied and unable to concentrate, or if you cut class to spend time with her, you have not yet developed mature love.

But if you study together, ask each other about work, and motivate each other to do well, you may have found love. Encouraging each other in the basic efforts of life is the core of marital happiness.

5. Can we work together? True love makes the mundane marvelous. The day-to-day tasks become fun when you do them with someone you love. Do you cooperate? Do you compliment rather than pout when she does better than you? Can you take instructions from each other? These are important love skills!

6. Are our relationships with other people better? True love makes it easier to get along with everyone in your life: friends, family members, teammates, and enemies. If your other relationships are neglected or strained, you have obsession, not love. One who truly loves you will get to know the people in your life, will grow to love them, will help you communicate with them, and will want you to spend time with them.

7. Do we demonstrate our respect and admiration for each other? True love shows itself in action. Does he include you in conversations even when his friends are around? Does he listen to and consider your ideas? Is he willing to learn from you? Does he show excitement over your accomplishments? Is he sensitive to your moods and needs? Does he proudly introduce you to his family and friends? Does he know just what to say and do to make you feel good about yourself? These indicate love.

8. Do we trust each other? Jealousy may seem romantic, but it demonstrates a lack of trust. True love gives the other person freedom to get to know other people, to spend time alone, and to think for oneself. Confidence in each other's care keeps you from worrying when a potential competitor comes along.

9. Do we both give equally to the relationship? True love is mutual. Each does some of the giving and some of the receiving. He talks some of the time, and she listens some of the time. She brags on him, and he brags on her. She does what he wants to do, and he does what she wants to do. Each learns to detect the other person's feelings and ask about them. When one does most of the giving or most of the taking, its abuse, not love.

10. Can we solve problems? All relationships have problems. Only people who solve relational problems can stay together. True love swallows its pride, refuses to attack the other, and sometimes does more than its share. How do you solve your problems now? How well can you negotiate, listen to each other's side of the story, consider each other's feelings? Do each of you compromise, or does one demand her way? The quality of your problem-solving skills is a good predictor of marital success.

11. Do we enjoy each other? Love means you want to be with each other more than anyone else in the world. A clue that you are right for each other is that each time together is a new adventure. Do you continue to learn from each other and about each other? Is there always something more to talk about?

12. Do I want to commit myself to this person no matter what happens? You promise "for better and for worse" during the wedding ceremony. Of course, you want the "for betters" like romantic evenings, working toward mutual goals, talking, and sharing. But think about some of the "for worses" most marriages encounter. Decide how well the two of you might face them: *You wreck his new car; she has to work late; the baby is crying at 3:00 AM and he won't take his turn with her; both of you want to go to your own parents' homes for Christmas; there's only enough money to buy what one of you wants; he complains about the meal you spent all day cooking; you have the stomach flu; his job moves you away from your friends.* Can the two of you work through these problems? Are you willing to rekindle the fires of love when the romance fades (and it will)? If so, you'll build the happiest and marriage ever. This #12 is the ultimate love question: Will both of you commit yourself to the other for the rest of your lives, for better and for worse? This is love.

Think: What if you and your sweetheart have eleven of the above twelve indicators of true love? Find out why, and grow the twelfth before you marry!

Read On: First John 4:16-21 and 1 Corinthians 13:4-8 describe God's kind of love. Which of these characteristics are present in your relationship?

Challenge: You may have all the indications of love but not be ready for marriage because of age, school, or other factors. Rather than dwell on marriage, concentrate on deepening your relationship. How can you communicate more clearly, solve problems more effectively, and show you care more firmly?

Me First

To truly be in love, you must first love yourself. Until you find happiness as a single person, you cannot love a sweetheart.

"Isn't that kind of conceited? I thought love meant to forget yourself and concentrate on others."

Love does mean forgetting yourself to concentrate on others. But to do that you must be secure enough to let yourself go. The source of that security is Jesus Christ. Jesus emphasized God's command to "love your fellowman as yourself" (Mark 12:31). Whether we try or not, we obey this command. We treat others the way we feel about ourselves:

Those who like themselves . . .	*Those who hate themselves . . .*
Focus on others	Feel self-conscious
Treat others with respect	Treat others rudely
Notice other's good points	Notice other's bad points
Disagree but still love	Lash out and criticize
Congratulate your success	Feel threatened by your success
Show interest	List their achievements
Feel confident	Feel insecure
Compliment others	Put others down
Consider another's opinion	Call the other wrong

Loving yourself is not conceited. Conceited people hide behind a facade of self-love. When you truly love yourself, you don't have to prove it to anyone. You know your faults (Ps. 51:3) and work toward changing them (Ps. 51:10).

William notices when Sara does something extra, like fixing her hair the way he likes it or listening to his story. William is free to talk about and show his feelings—he cried once when he lost the scholarship. He appreciates Sara's feelings too, even the negative ones like anger and frustration. William understands Sara's need for her girl friends and guy friends. When she's busy, he finds something else to do, even if it's sitting home alone reading. At parties they sometimes don't even sit together. But they know they'll leave together. When they have a problem, they attack the problem, not each other.

Why does William have so much trust in Sara? What makes their relationship go so smoothly? William likes William. Because he does, he is free to love others. He can love as he loves himself.

Russel demands Tamara's constant attention. He expects her to be ready whenever he calls and seldom lets her know his plans ahead of time. At first Tamara was impressed that he liked her so much. But lately she feels controlled. Russel insists that he have the last word in every conversation and pouts whenever Tamara disagrees with him. When she talks with anyone but him, he furiously accuses her of betrayal. He freely criticizes her, expecially when problems arise, "If you loved me the way a good woman should, we wouldn't have these problems!"

Obviously, Russel is the one with problems. He is so consumed with proving his own manhood that he refuses to give Tamara the freedom to enjoy life. He can't love her because he hasn't learned to love himself. Until Russel learns that Russel is lovable, he cannot love Tamara, nor can he trust her love for him. Russel loves Tamara the way he loves himself: very poorly.

Yes, it's OK to like yourself. In fact, it's essential!

Think: We all know people who put up with Russel's treatment. How can we like ourselves well enough to neither put up with nor dish out this treatment? What would you advise Tamara to do?

Read On: Bible verses which describe God's love for you include: John 3:16; 1 John 3:1; 1 John 4:7-12; Hebrews 4:16; 1 Peter 5:7. Love yourself the way God loves you! See pages 65-66.

So Is It Love?

Determining whether you're in love becomes easier when you:

Give it time: It takes time to get to know someone, to learn how well you get along. Take all the time you need. Most people feel you need at least a year and then an engagement of several months. The best relationships develop slowly.

Give it experience: Spend time together in as many different settings as possible. The greater variety of your experiences, the better you will understand the way the two of you respond to each other, to problems, to joys. You will better understand how happy you'll be in marriage. See Chapter 4 for over fifty things to do together.

Give it nurture: When you're in love, everything seems so right with the world. Keep that goodness growing by daily finding new ways to show your sweetheart you care. See pages 37 and 51 for starter ideas. Let your love spill over into other relationships. Get to know other people as a couple and as individuals. See each new relationship as an opportunity to learn how to love and to teach what you know.

Give it evaluation: What do other people say about your relationship? Check with people who know you well. Ask your friends, parents, and adults with happy marriages: What do you like/not like about Daniel? Do you think he's good for me? What strengths do you see in our relationship? What weaknesses? How do we encourage or frustrate each other? Does it look like love? Proverbs 11:14 and 12:15 explain that deciding by yourself is risky. Seeking good advice helps you recognize the right choice.

Give it prayer: Only God knows who is the best marriage partner for you. Talk your relationship over with Him at all stages. Ask Him to help you separate the permanent from the temporary, the truth from the deception. Trust Him to guide you as you look for the best person possible.

11
Breaking Up: Minimize The Pain

When you begin to date someone, you will either marry that someone or break up with him. Because most of us date several people before choosing the one we marry, most of us will face at least one breakup. Breaking up hurts horribly. How can you minimize the pain and maybe even grow through it?

First: Realize that God understands: *"The Lord is near to the brokenhearted, and saves the crushed in spirit"* (Ps. 34:18, RSV). Let God's love bring you through the pain and fill your emptiness.

Second: Be assured that your pain will not last forever. You will feel better. Love pain hurts but it also heals.

Third: Know that God promises to take even the most painful experiences and use them for good (Rom. 8:28). Ask Him what you can learn through the breakup. Ask God's guidance as you move into His next step for your life. See 9 under "And When You're Broken Up With . . ." in this chapter.

Youth suggest these guidelines for breaking up:

• Refuse to ignore relationship problems: don't play games or try to hide your feelings. Be honest with yourself.

• Pray about what you should say and for her understanding.

• Be honest and sensitive toward the one you're breaking up with. This makes it easier for his feelings to heal.

• Tell him yourself rather than relying on another person to tell him for you. Tell him in person, not by phone or letter.

• Understand she may feel hurt and not want to talk for awhile.

95

• Break up before the other person becomes more interested than you are. The longer you date, the harder it is to break up.

Tips for the Breaker Upper

Joel is thinking, *Irene has been so special to me. I can't bear to hurt her by telling her how I really feel. Maybe if I just back off slowly, she won't hurt as badly.*

But Irene is thinking, *I know its coming. Joel has been distant and preoccupied. He doesn't call as often. When we're together, he doesn't look me in the eye. Joel's phone is busy a lot, so I imagine he's already calling other girls. Why doesn't he just tell me? Not knowing what's going on is driving me crazy!*

There is no way to "keep from hurting" the one with whom you break up. Anytime you have been dating awhile, breaking up will hurt. But you'll inflict more pain if you ignore the problem. A clean, direct break will hurt less and heal easier.

1. Be direct but gentle: "I hate to tell you this, but I think its time to break up. It hurts me to hurt you, but it won't help you or me to pretend."

2. Tell the reason if you know it: "I'm feeling trapped and want more freedom. I want more time with friends, and I want to date other people."

3. Concentrate on your problems, not hers: "I want you to know that you've done nothing to make me feel this way. I've just discovered a restlessness in myself that I have to settle."

4. But mention her problems if they are serious: "I need to tell you that your fiery temper is one reason we can't go on. I'd rather talk out problems. Yelling and throwing frightens me."

Hint: Do this with caution! When personality problems have caused the break up, mentioning them might give the person the courage to change. But you aren't always the best one to do it!

5. Add a little sugar with the medicine: "I have always liked your sincerity. You have taught me a lot about being real."

It feels horrible to be rejected via a breakup. When you tell her what you like about her, she'll remember her value.

6. Give her time to respond. "Is there anything you want to say? I hate to dump all this on you and you not say anything. I want to know your thoughts and feelings too." Then listen!

7. Give hope only if it is real. "While you're at college I want us to be free to date other people. At the end of the year, I wouldn't be surprised if we still like each other best!"

If you have no plans to date her again, say so positively: "I hope things go great for you. Thanks for being part of my life."

8. Avoid, "Let's be friends." Instead say something like, "I care about you even though we won't be dating. I'm glad we've shared such good experiences. You've helped me grow."

It's nearly impossible to gear down dating feelings to friendship feelings. Of course, you'll still care, but its usually wise not to see each other for awhile. "Let's be friends" gives her hope for continuing the relationship. She'll heal more easily if you aren't around. Give each other several weeks or months before you try to reestablish a friendship.

9. Expect some pain. Even though you're doing the breaking up, you'll still miss her. Missing doesn't mean you were wrong to break up; it means you are changing your life and she's no longer a part of it. Every experience you shared bound you together. The longer you dated the harder it is to unbind and the longer you'll miss her.

10. Make it a clean break. Even if you sincerely feel that you were wrong to break up, don't get back together right away. Give yourself about a month before dating her again. This will give you time to sort out the normal breakup feelings from the conviction that God wants you to get back together.

Challenge: Ephesians 4:29 says, "Do not use harmful words, but only helpful words, the kind that build up and provide what is needed, so that what you say will do good to those who hear you." List words that would "do good" to someone you are breaking up with.

And When You're Broken Up With . . .

1. Listen without interrupting. Its almost as hard to do the breaking

up as it is to receive it. Hear him out to understand the reasons for the break up.

2. Ask questions. "Is there something I did to cause this breakup?" "Do you think we need to just give each other a few months apart, or do you see this as permanent?" Whatever you don't understand, ask. Realize that he may not fully understand his reasons and that's OK.

3. Let him go. You're crazy about him and you want to hang on. That's normal, but it won't work. You may be convinced that he's making a big mistake and that the two of you are meant to stay together. And you may be right. But the best way to find that out is to let him go. Freedom helps you both know the direction your futures should take.

Hint: If he decides he wants to date you again shortly after the breakup, it's usually wise to wait. A breakup signals something important and should not be taken lightly. Give yourself time to think and decide before dating him again.

4. Let yourself go. You'll experience intense feelings, and it's OK to let them all out, even if it means crying in front of the person who has just broken up with you.

5. Talk out your feelings with someone you trust. You may feel lonely, angry, hurt, vengeful, and hopeless. Let yourself feel these feelings, and then talk them out. Talk with yourself, talk with God, and talk with friends. Focus on yourself long enough to heal your pain but not long enough to bask in self-pity.

6. Refuse to hold a grudge or get revenge. Because you hurt, you want to hurt back. More drastic ways to get revenge include violence toward your ex-sweetheart or violence toward yourself (suicide). Neither these nor such calmer forms as rumor spreading or gossip will help. When you feel like getting revenge, talk about it rather than do it. Love easily turns to hate when you're hurt. Refuse to let this happen to you. It will only make your pain worse. As hard as it is, continue to treat your ex-sweetheart as a person of worth.

7. Resist the temptation to withdraw. "I'll never trust again!" Withdrawal guarantees that you'll never have to break up, but it doesn't

mean you'll never hurt. Continual loneliness is much more painful than a possible breakup. After giving yourself some time to recover, begin going out with friends and begin to open yourself up to new sweethearts. Pray for God's guidance.

8. Resist the urge to quickly find another sweetheart. It's OK to date right away, but don't jump into a steady relationship. Your emotions need time to heal before they're ready to blend again. You risk using someone when you date too soon after a breakup.

9. Evaluate. Ask yourself: What could I do differently next time to help the relationship last? What did I learn about the type of person I chose to date? What different qualities do I want next time? How can I notice the good and bad in a person before we date? What did I learn about myself? What did I learn about how to communicate, solve problems, and show care?

10. Pray for God's will. What does God want next? He may have someone even better for you. He may want you back with the original sweetheart, after you've both changed a bit. He may want you to concentrate on friends for awhile. Pray that you'll understand God's leading and recognize the person He has for you.

Signals that a Breakup Might Be Necessary

You like someone else. This is probably the most popular reason people break up. Liking someone else often means that the one you're dating isn't the right one for you. The only way to find out is to date or get to know that other person.

You fight more than you have fun. Everyone disagrees from time to time. But do you fight out your disagreements rather than talk them out? How do the two of you handle angry feelings? A healthy couple can admit them, talk about them, and heal them. If you two can't, you're not right for each other.

Your sweetheart brings out the worst in you. Is it harder to get along with people after you've been with him? Does he frustrate you more than encourage you? Are you less willing to obey God and your parents when you're with him? Do you spend less time with your friends? If so, he's not good for you.

You're involved physically beyond your emotional, social, and spiritual closeness. If you have trouble thinking of things to talk about but no trouble making out, your relationship is weak. If you cannot talk, solve problems, enjoy being together in groups, motivate each other to obey God, or share your feelings, your relationship won't make it. Back off from the physical or back off from each other.

You are a Christian, but your sweetheart is not. There is no way you can be compatible if you are not alike in your beliefs about God. "God won't mind if I date him. The only thing wrong with him is that he's not a Christian!" you rationalize. But the Bible is clear—2 Corinthians 6:14 warns against close relationships with people who are unbelievers. Choose a sweetheart who not only believes in God but lets God guide his life. They're out there!

You're not sure you want to spend the rest of your life with this person. If other people begin to attract you and you feel restless, discover what it means. You may just be bored and need to spice up your present relationship. Attention, not a breakup, is the cure for this ailment. But if you've discovered that you are not as compatible as you once thought, if you don't meet each other's needs as fully as you had hoped, if you have nothing new to say to each other, you may need to break up. Dating others is one way to confirm or defeat your suspicions.

Hint: Be genuine with this type of breakup: "This sounds like a line, but I really do need some time to date others. I may find that you are the one I'm searching for or I may not. I pray that God will make it clear what He wants for us. Let's talk again in three months to decide what to do. Please date others too."

The person is treating you poorly. Never put up with being used, with physical abuse, or with emotional torment. Once you see this tendency, talk about it. If the abuse does not stop and stay stopped, break things off immediately. Love yourself enough to find someone who loves you. See Chapter 4.

You'll be apart. Distance is hard on relationships. Moving to another community may necessitate breaking up. Give each other freedom to date other people, agreeing to keep in touch and see each other when you're in town. This breakup often has hope. Many couples discover that they find no one better than their sweetheart back home. Other times one finds a new sweetheart. Freedom demonstrates the relationship's strength.

But Why Can't I Do It?

Perhaps you're in one of the above situations. You know you need to break up, but you just can't bring yourself to do it. Notice these barriers and overcome them:

—You've grown accustomed to each other. When you think about breaking up, your good times seem to overshadow the bad. You don't want to miss him. Familiarity is keeping you from trying someone new. Was there really more good than bad?

—You fear being alone. Loneliness sounds less bearable than miserable togetherness. But only when you let yourself be lonely for awhile can you find someone new.

—You don't want to hurt him. You wouldn't have gone out with him unless you liked him. Its hard to hurt someone you like, even when that hurt is less than the pain of staying together.

—You worry that something is wrong with you when you can't keep a relationship together. But that's seldom the case.

Dating takes time and sorting out. In the future you can get to know people as friends before dating them. This helps you avoid repeated breakups and helps you feel better about yourself.

Be Good to Yourself and Good to Your Dates

From beginning to end, respect the needs and feelings of your dates and yourself. Because you influence everyone you date, and they influence you, take dating seriously. Once you've dated someone, that person remains a part of your life. Stay in constant touch with God and the people who know you to decide whom to date, how close to grow to the people you date, and when a breakup is necessary. Remember that you are God's masterpiece.

If and when a breakup comes, work through your feelings until you can look back on the experience without bitterness or anger. The way you respond to breakup pain can make or break the way your future relationships grow. Let each relationship enrich all others. (A negative relationship can show you what you don't want!) Let your dating goal be a lifelong and happy marriage.

When you go through a breakup, remember that God is still in control. Read and reread these promises:

"I alone know the plans I have for you, plans to bring you prosperity and not disaster, plans to bring about the future you hope for" (Jer. 29:11).

"Seek your happiness in the Lord, and he will give you your heart's desire. . . . "Be patient and wait for the Lord to act; . . . Don't give in to worry or anger; it only leads to trouble" (Ps. 37:4,7,8).

12
Marriage: Recognize When You're Ready

"No marriage for me! I don't want to be tied down to the same person all my life. I want my freedom!" declared Lee.

"I can hardly wait till I get married!" countered Dana. *"What an adventure it will be—plenty of time to get to know each other, sexual freedom, sharing everything, working together toward the same goals, someone always there who understands me."*

"But, marriage just doesn't work anymore. With divorce rates as high as 50 percent, it's obvious that something is wrong with it," persisted Lee. *"I'll just live with someone until it ends and then move on."*

"I think marriages fail because people don't understand it. They think it's all romance. When problems come, they think they've married the wrong person. Any relationship has problems, and solving them is part of what makes marriage strong," said Dana. *"Besides, how would breaking up after living together be less painful than divorce?"*

"I wouldn't be 'divorced.' I suppose the pain would be the same," admitted Lee. *"But don't you think that divorce shows we're more honest? People used to stay together and be miserable. Now we're free to move on to something better."*

"But is there anything better? I think most of the time divorce and remarriage simply exchanges one set of problems for another," said Dana. *"Wouldn't it be easier to work things out with one person than to break up over and over?"*

"I do have to admit that breaking up devastates me," said Lee. *"I tend to get really attached to someone, and breaking up seems to tear*

*out a part of me. I feel so rejected, so empty. I certainly don't want to
face a lifetime of that!"*

*"God gave us that need to be united with someone. Breaking up a
marriage is never His perfect will. I think marriage can work if we find
someone who's willing to persist through troubles and keep love growing,"* said Dana. *"Just think, no more breaking up!*

Think: Why do you want to marry or not marry? What are some
good and bad reasons to marry?

What Is Marriage?

Marriage is a friendship, a creation, a workshop, a team effort, and
a picture of Christ and the church.

"My husband is my best friend. We still have romance, but things
seem more secure, more steady. Everything's an adventure because we
do it together. We understand each other and know how to make each
other happy. I can relax so completely when he's around. I'd never
make it without his loving encouragement."

"The first year we were married we were convinced we'd married
the wrong person! I think we were just both so independent that we
had trouble getting used to considering someone else. But God has
helped us create a great marriage. We talk about everything, and we're
learning how to identify and solve problems before they get too big.
Our marriage gets better every year!"

"Our marriage is like a workshop: She whittles off my rough edges,
and I sand her smooth. When you're married to someone, you have
to learn to get along. We've tried to get rid of our bad habits to keep
from hurting each other. Because we care, we give a lot. And as a
result, we become better people. Getting along really well with your
marriage partner improves the way you get along with everybody
else."

"We were in constant conflict for awhile. We finally realized that
if we'd just work with each other rather than against each other we'd
accomplish more. We discovered the beauty of teamwork, give and
take, mutual support, and understanding. Now we work toward the

same goals and concentrate on discovering and meeting each others' needs. We love each other more each day."

"Ultimately, marriage is to be a picture of Christ's relationship with the church. Obedience to Christ, submission, spiritual leadership, love, respect, and unity are just a few of the characteristics of Christian marriage. It takes a while to develop these qualities, but to see them in action is beautiful."

Read On: Marriage is compared to the relationship between Jesus Christ and the church in Ephesians 5:21-33.

Are We Compatible?

"How can I be sure the one I want to marry is the right one?" No one set of factors guarantees success in marriage. But couples with the following characteristics tend to stay happy.

• Both are Christians. Because God created marriage, it makes sense that the best marriages are the ones guided by Him. Choose not only a Christian but a growing Christian, one whose beliefs closely match yours. Find someone who encourages your faith.

• Both are willing to Work. The best marriages are not 50-50, they're 100-100. Both partners must be willing to give everything they have to make the marriage succeed. What does your sweetheart do to help your relationship now? Marriage gets tough, and only those committed to give will make it.

• Each is like the other. The saying "opposites attract" applies to magnets, not relationships. Though different people are intriguing, the chances of smooth relating are slim. Each difference means something to overcome. When you list your similarities and differences, the similarities should win.

• Each depends on the other. In a healthy marriage, each partner needs the other. This is called *interdependence*. As 1 Corinthians 11:11 explains, "In Christ's fellowship woman is as essential to man as man to woman" (NEB). Husbands and wives depend on each other for encouragement, understanding, advice, and support. And both depend on God.

• Each says "I love you" in many ways. Romantic words and

sexual love are only two of the hundreds of ways to say, "I love you." Helping each other with chores, taking time together, smiling at the right moment, stopping to listen, understanding feelings, refraining from ridicule, complementing privately and publicly, refusing to criticize the other in front of someone, and calling when you're late are a few.

• Each makes decisions with the other. Marriage presents big and little decisions almost continually: Where shall we live? What kind of house do we want? What job shall I take? Shall we have children? When? Which bologna shall we buy? What church shall we join? What show shall we watch? Each decision gives you opportunity to grow closer or to fight. Happily married couples share their ideas and find an answer that pleases both.

• Each encourages the other. "I know you can do it!" "How are you feeling about the competition tomorrow?" "Did you and your mom talk?" "What did your teacher say about your paper?" Happy marriages grow when each knows the other cares.

• Each accepts the other. "He'll change after I marry him." "Once we get married it will be better." Not so! People do not change for the better after marriage. In fact, you usually find more that frustrates you! Happily married couples chose someone they already like rather than someone they can fix to suit them.

Think: When youth were asked, "Who would make the ideal mate?" they listed these characteristics: Christian, honest, sincere, encouraging, respectful, sensitive, understanding, open, shares responsibility, unselfish, and appreciative. How does your date match up? If your sweetheart (present or future) were evaluating you, which qualities would he say you possess? Work right now on developing these qualities.

Role Play

Who should do what in a marriage? Using this list for ideas, jot down tasks you want to do. Cross out ones you refuse to do. Ask your sweetheart to do the same and then compare lists.

take out the garbage	cook	wash dishes
send birthday cards	vaccuum	clean bathrooms
earn money	budget money	change diapers
buy clothes	mow the lawn	week/trim lawn
care for children	buy groceries	clean the house
fix broken things	mend	select furniture
pay bills	run errands	make appointments
balance the checkbook	wash clothes	get the mail

Did you discover any chores that neither of you wants to do? Any that you both want to do? Some that only men should do? Some that only women should do? Talk about how you would work out these conflicts. Somebody has to take out the garbage and clean the commodes. Maybe you can split these distasteful tasks or find some way to make them adventuresome.

"We agreed to share equally, but as soon as our baby was born, he announced that he didn't change diapers!" To anticipate problems like these, reread the list of duties. Which did your mother do? Which did your father do? You tend to do what your matching parent did.

"But I don't mind changing the diapers and cleaning house. I'm glad to do that while my husband earns the money!" And that's great! The important thing is that you agree on the way you'll share the daily tasks of life. They can make or break a marriage. Prayer, cooperation, and communication will keep these little things from becoming big problems.

Become Like My Parents?

You unconsciously imitate your parents' marriage skills because you were exposed to them daily. This can be good or bad, depending on how well they talk and listen, solve conflict, and demonstrate love to each other. Watch your own and your date's parents. How does his dad relate to his mom? What is supper conversation like? You'll tend to become like your matching parent.

"But I don't want to end up like my mom!" And you don't have to! The good news is that God is in the redeeming business. God can

transform the negative characteristics we have learned from our parents into positive ones. This change seldom happens instantly or easily. But commitment to God and deciding to change are first steps.

Consider Rachel's story:

Rachel's mother criticized Rachel's father to others but would never tell him her concerns. Rachel learned her lessons well. Though she never said anything unkind to people, she criticized them behind their backs. Though Rachel had vowed not to criticize the way her mother did, she noticed the pattern developing.

Rachel talked with God and her husband about her desire to work with her husband rather than against him. She decided that she would tell him her complaints, not someone else. She vowed never to say anything negative about him to another person. Gradually she began to see the good in her husband, and they got along better. Her husband became her best friend.

Challenge: List the characteristics in your parents that bug you. Now look for hints of those same characteristics in yourself. Talk with God about specific ways He could help you transform those negative characteristics into positive ones.

List also the positive characteristics you have learned from your parents. Thank God for teaching you through your parents.

Divorce: Will It Happen to Me?

"Both our parents had divorced, so we knew the desperate pain that both the parents and children feel. We decided that we weren't going to go through that again. We were going to be different and make our marriage last. That's where our commitment came in. Commitment is sticking through what you don't want to go through. Your feelings for each other may vary many times when you're married, and only commitment keeps you coming back to each other. Often I don't like my wife because of something she does or the mood I'm in, but we renew our marriage vows every day. Commitment kept us together. It's been hard, but we've both worked at it, and we've made it."

As this person suggests, marriage grows a little bit every day, either closer or further apart. Happy marriages grow steadily closer. Divorce comes when couples grow so far apart they don't know how to get back together. Marriage is like a garden: partners must cultivate love and pull the weeds of separation. As you date and marry, use your words to grow understanding, communication, and cooperation. Weed out accusation, criticism, neglect, and fighting.

Cultivate	Weed Out
"That makes sense."	"That's a dumb idea."
"What do you think?"	"We'll do it my way."
"Tell me about it."	"I don't have time to listen."
"How can I help?"	"Why do you do such stupid things?"
"I need you to . . ."	"Why don't you ever . . .?"
"It bothers me when you . . ."	"You always . . ."
"Its hard on both of us."	"Why do you do this to me?"
"I'm sorry."	"It's all your fault."
"Can we compromise?"	"We'll never work it out!"
"Let's start again."	"This is the last straw!"

Think: What actions might match these words? How well do you and your sweetheart cultivate love? Separation?

A recently divorced woman suggested: *"Know about divorce before you marry, not as an option but to prevent it. The feelings of failure, disappointment, and rejection are devastating. And those feelings affect not only you and your ex-spouse but your children, your friends, your parents, and so many others. We think divorce is a matter between two married people, but it's not that easy. Divorce is usually selfish: What will make me happy? rather than, 'What will grow this relationship?' If love was there at first, it can always be revived. When you enter marriage, agree that when trouble comes, you'll solve it, not run from it. Both of you have to agree to stick it out no matter what happens. If only one is committed, it will never work.*

"When you're in love, you can't imagine ever breaking up, but

examine factors like how much time you spend together, how well you talk out disagreements, how much give and take there is. Don't marry someone unless these factors are present."

Someone has said, *"Knowing divorce is possible makes us work to prevent it."* You don't keep divorce away by ignoring it, but by building a strong marriage. You agree that divorce will not be an option for you, and you build security in your marriage by consistent loving actions and constant communication. Talk out your conflicts and rejoice in your successes. Grow closer every day until you are inseparable friends.

Isn't It OK to Marry a Non-Christian if We Love Each Other?

"He's not a Christian now, but I know he will become one after we marry."

When you are eager to make things work, you can convince yourself that your non-Christian sweetheart will one day become a Christian. Though this can happen, it is unlikely. Those who reject Christianity in their teen years tend to stay resistant.

Rochelle felt convicted to give part of her money to feed the hungry. She felt this would be a way to love as Jesus loves. When she suggested it to Nathan, he responded, "I break my back trying to feed our family. Why do you keep trying to give away my money? That church puts crazy ideas in your head."

Obviously Rochelle hesitated to obey God in this matter. Because she loved Nathan, she wanted to please him. Because Nathan was not a Christian, pleasing him often conflicted with serving God.

Don't put yourself into a situation where you have to choose between two important loves: God and your spouse. As hard as it is, break up with the non-Christian and search for a spouse who loves both God and you. The pain you experience now will be small compared to a lifetime of frustration.

A Christian married to a non-Christian for twenty years explained: *"I'd give anything to be able to share with my husband the way I share with other Christians. Anytime I talk about religion he clams up. It gets so tense I just don't bring it up. We're just not close like we used to be.*

Marrying a Christian doesn't guarantee a happy marriage, but it increases your chances. Not marrying a Christian almost certainly guarantees failure!"

Prepare for a Super Marriage

Preparation for marriage begins now. What you do today and tomorrow affects your marriage.

1. *Practice relating to people.* Learn how to create more happiness than frustration. Discern people's moods and how to respond to them. Learn to communicate, solve problems, listen, and understand. Marriage is a skill, and you can excel!

Read On: The book *Friends: Finding and Keeping Them* (Broadman Press, 1985) details how to grow relationship skills.

2. *Watch and imitate happily married couples.* Ask these couples to share their secrets for getting along and blending their relationship. What do they say and do to demonstrate love for each other? Tell them your ideas about love and marriage, and ask them to help you match your ideas to reality.

3. *Learn all you can.* As you read, meet people, watch movies, read books, notice the actions/words that bring about marital successes and failures. Make a point to develop the successful actions and omit the problem-causing actions.

4. *Focus on marriage rather than the wedding.* Weddings are delightfully fun—gifts, food, friends, and attention! The preparation and gifts can last for months. But then the marriage begins. And that marriage is a living, growing relationship that needs daily care. Like in a garden, both husband and wife have to keep pulling the weeds and nurturing the healthy parts. Working toward the tasty fruit can be fun. But sometimes its grueling work. True love finds this work worthwhile.

5. *Pray for wisdom in choosing.* You can do much to increase your chances of happy marriage (see Chapter 10). But because people change over the years and because we never truly know someone until we marry that person, only God knows the right person for you. Pray you'll hear and obey God's voice.

Challenge: One of the beauties of dating is freedom to find the one you want to marry. While dating, you can break up with someone who doesn't have the qualities you want. But once you marry, you no longer have that option. Don't settle for anyone who will not develop the marriage skills described in this chapter and in Chapter 10. Build the happiest marriage ever!